regina's vegetarian table

REGINA CAMPBELL

regina's vegetarian table

your invitation to flavor, freshness, and health

PRIMA PUBLISHING

Published by Prima Publishing, Roseville, California. Member of the Crown Publishing Group, a division of Random House, Inc.

PRIMA PUBLISHING and colophon are trademarks of Random House, Inc., registered with the United States Patent and Trademark Office.

Interior Design by Mary Beth Salmon
Interior Illustrations by Melissa Sweet
Food Stylist: Sue White
Photography by Rose Hodges

On the Cover: Asparagus–Mushroom Quiche (pages 230–231), Asian Pear and Strawberry Salad (page 45), and Tomato Bruschetta (page 15).

Library of Congress Cataloging-in-Publication Data

Campbell, Regina.
    Regina's vegetarian table : your invitation to flavor, freshness, and health / Regina Campbell.
        p.   cm.
    Includes index.
    ISBN 0-7615-0697-7
    ISBN 0-7615-6370-9 (pbk.)
    1. Vegetarian cookery. I. Title.
TX837.C327 1997
641.5'636—dc20   97-39849
                                                              CIP

02 03 04 05 06 HH 10 9 8 7 6 5 4 3 2 1
Printed in the United States of America
First Paperback Edition

Visit us online at www.primapublishing.com

This is dedicated to Mom,

who lives in our hearts

as the best cook our little

palates ever knew.

contents

foreword

as a nonvegetarian, I consider Regina's attitude toward vegetarianism to be remarkably balanced and harmonious in its approach to life. As a wine merchant, I, of course, was delighted with Regina's enthusiastic embrace of wine as part of her vegetarian diet. It certainly made her appear more "mainstream" to me.

Regina's continuing enthusiasm for wine in moderation as part of her diet is supported by the Oldways Vegetarian Diet Pyramid, which recommends moderate wine intake on a daily basis as an optional part of an overall healthful diet. (Oldways, a Boston-based nonprofit group, was called a "food-issues think tank" by *Newsweek*, and has also published the Mediterranean and Asian Diet Pyramids.)

Regina's Vegetarian Table will appeal to the nonvegetarian because it removes the perceived intimidation of a vegetarian menu as "just too much trouble." The results are vegetarian dishes that are extraordinarily flavorful and easy to create. There is both convenience and accessibility to Regina's recipes.

My wine suggestions are intended to travel the same avenues of easy access and convenience, which means they are fairly general in nature with an emphasis on availability. The recommendations are primarily *varietal* (name of the primary grape used to make the wine), and may therefore seem somewhat repetitive. Keep in mind that specific wine recommendations would be instantly out of date following the publication of this book and would vary according to the success of subsequent vintages for that wine. To help you select the most complementary wine for a particular dish or menu, I have in some instances included descriptions associated with wine—for example, a crisp, light Chardonnay as opposed to an oaky, full-flavored Chardonnay or a fruity, tropical-flavored Chardonnay.

It is also important to remember that these generalized suggestions are just that—suggestions. I have enjoyed many dishes with wines that, well, were probably inappropriate but tasted good. Remember, in the world of wine there are no absolutes! Today we benefit from a refreshing attitude emphasizing the enjoyment of those wines that most appeal to us. Certainly that is part of the excitement in the expanding world of wine—freedom from old rules that allows us to experiment and enjoy our own preferences.

Salute!

David E. Berkley
Nationally recognized wine expert and consultant to the White House

acknowledgments

many influences enter into our experience of eating and creating food. As with many of us, my experience began with Mom. My only regret was how we shunned her culinary experiments growing up. Not until my son Stuart began turning his nose up at virtually all my culinary offerings in favor of anything that could be ordered at a drive-through window did I truly appreciate my mother's efforts. Now that she has returned to that great buffet in the sky, I spend my time discussing, creating, and eating food with my sister Denise and many good friends.

Since I'm better at cooking than paperwork, I owe many thanks to Gail Berman and Cindy Adkins Fong for helping turn my many loose notes into a book. Part of the motivation for writing this book was to ensure that I could find my favorite recipes when I needed them!

Special thanks also to Eric for getting the ball rolling, to Dan for sacrificing himself as the human guinea pig, and to Kurt, Linda, and Fred for all the encouragement during my shift to vegetarianism.

A very special thank you to David Berkley for taking the time from his busy schedule to select the wines for the main dishes and soup sections of this book. As wine consultant to the current and last two White House administrations, David is a rare talent in his field.

Also, many thanks to Jan Tilmon and Jennifer Basye Sander for bringing this project to print.

And finally, I'd like to thank my father for a lifetime of keeping his nose to the grindstone, which allowed me the period of grace to make some dreams come true.

introduction

notice what happens to your senses when you walk down a supermarket produce aisle, or better yet, through a farmer's market. The colors, smells, and textures come alive and awaken something primitive in us: Memories of the bursting sweetness of watermelon and peaches in summer, the cinnamony scent of apple crisp on a cold winter night, onions and garlic in the frying pan, about to transform just about any dish into something delicious and memorable. All of these earthly works of art await, sun-drenched and laden with rich nutrients.

Whatever your reason for turning to a fresher and lighter diet, the objective of this book is to make your transition as easy as possible. As a working mother, I don't have time to jump through hoops to make a fresh and great tasting meal. Indeed, time seems to be the one thing all of us are running short of. But that doesn't mean we must sacrifice our health or the pleasure of eating.

As you go through the recipes in this book, you will see that I have taken shortcuts in preparation wherever possible. But, I guarantee, nothing has been given up in the flavor of the end product. As you prepare the recipes, I encourage you to add, subtract, and make them your own. Soon you will wonder how anyone could have ever asked the question, "What do vegetarians eat anyway?"

uncommon foods commonly used in vegetarian cooking

Many of the following foods are only used as options in this cookbook. The basic recipes call for common ingredients that can be found easily in supermarkets. Where dairy products are used, cow's milk is the basic ingredient called for. But many people are moving away from cow's milk, substituting it with other types of milk or milk-free products. Information about some of these cow's milk substitutes, as well as other dietary options, follows.

GOAT'S MILK • Goat's milk is sometimes tolerated by those who cannot drink cow's milk, making it popular among the health conscious. Though whole goat's milk is slightly higher in fat than whole cow's milk, the smaller size of the fat globules in goat's milk may contribute to its digestibility. Keep it properly refrigerated to avoid a "goaty" flavor or odor.

MISO • This soybean paste has been used as part of the Japanese diet for 13 centuries and is packed with nutrition. Miso is made by cooking soybeans in salt water then inoculating them with a bacterial culture. This culture breaks down the soybeans, and any grains that may accompany it, into a flavorful paste that is rich in protein, minerals, and B vitamins, is low in fat, and contains no cholesterol. The bacterial culture in miso also aids in digestion and may enhance the immune system against some bacterial diseases. You can add it to soups, stews, and sauces. Miso is generally found in the refrigerated section of health food stores.

NOTE • Miso is very salty, so those on a sodium-restricted diet need to use it sparingly.

SOY MILK • People wishing to cut down on their intake of saturated fats, or those who cannot tolerate cow's milk, will find a refreshing alternative in soy milk. While plain soy milk has considerably less calcium than cow's milk, it contains more protein and iron with fewer calories and less fat. Some varieties used as a beverage are flavored with unrefined sweeteners. Soy milk can be substituted for cow's milk in most recipes.

NOTE • This pertains to *whole* soy milk, as half of the protein is found in the fat. Conversely, cow's milk provides higher amounts of protein with a lower fat content, but only slightly.

SHOYU • Shoyu is the queen of soy sauces. Its four main ingredients are soybeans, wheat, water, and salt. Naturally fermented, shoyu takes two years to make. The result is a much richer soy sauce than is found in the common supermarket varieties. While shoyu is commonly available in health food stores, you may have to shop around to find it in the supermarket. It costs a little more, but it's well worth the investment.

TAHINI • Tahini is an all-natural creamy purée of sesame seeds. As with nut butters, tahini is high in fat, containing 100 calories per tablespoon. To its credit, however, sesame tahini is very high in calcium, potassium, magnesium, and vitamin A, as well as protein. Tahini is normally used in small amounts and adds a distinct, rich flavor to Middle Eastern dishes.

TEMPEH • Tempeh is a pressed, fermented soybean cake, produced by exposing soybeans to a friendly bacterial culture. The bacterial fermentation of tempeh creates its unique flavor and makes the soybeans easier to digest. Very high in protein, with levels equal to that of chicken or beef, tempeh has none of the saturated fat or cholesterol of its meat-based counterparts. Suitable for baking, frying, and using in sauces or soups, tempeh's versatility makes it an important part of the vegetarian diet.

TOFU • Tofu is also known as bean curd. It is made by soaking whole soybeans, puréeing them in water, then cooking the purée in boiling water. The purée is strained and the remaining soy milk is curdled with a coagulant. The end product is a smooth, almost tasteless form of vegetable protein that is low in saturated fats and contains no cholesterol. Tofu will take on the flavor of any foods or spices you combine it with. You can usually find tofu in the produce or refrigerated section of your supermarket.

VEGETARIAN WORCESTERSHIRE SAUCE • The vegetarian version of this all-purpose sauce does not have quite the same bite as Lea & Perrins, but it does have a wonderfully smooth, spicy, full flavor. I find it a satisfactory substitute for the anchovy-laced original. Vegetarian Worcestershire can be found at some, but not all, health food stores.

fats and oils

Amid all of the concern over fats in the diet, some misunderstandings have occurred. Today many people think fat in the diet is a bad thing. In fact, the body needs certain kinds of "good" fats for most of its tasks, including maintaining a healthy heart, digestion, brain function, maintaining supple skin and hair, adrenal functioning, and energy production. The body needs fat so badly that it goes to great lengths to store fat for future use. The problems arise when we eat the wrong kinds of fats and do not balance them with "good" fats. Hydrogenated fats and fats that have been subjected to very high heat (for frying) would be considered detrimental. Eating too many hard saturated and monounsaturated fats without balancing them with vegetable fats is also unhealthful.

The secret is to enjoy a balanced and moderate consumption of fats in the diet. There are many books available on this subject that can help you determine how much fat and which kinds of fat you should consume in a day, week, or month. One book that is considered the most thorough on the subject is titled *Fats That Heal, Fats That Kill* by Dr. Udo Erasmus. Most nutritionists agree that olive oil is the queen of oils for all-purpose day-to-day use because of its ratio of monounsaturated fat to saturated fat. It also remains stable under heat better than many oils, making it ideal for cooking. This is actually not true. In fact, all oils are damaged and carry health risks when heated above 300 degrees Fahrenheit, i.e., the temperature required for frying and sautéing

NOTE • Except for extra-virgin olive oil, the oils that fill store shelves have all been stripped of nutrients and fried before they're even bottled. Healthful alternatives are available in brown glass bottles, refrigerated in health food stores. The store may have to order it for you.

OIL PRODUCTION • Most people don't know that the colorless, odorless, tasteless oils commonly found on store shelves have undergone extensive processing that you probably don't care to know about. But I should probably tell you anyway.

In short, after they've been pressed (this includes cold pressed oils), they are degummed (treated with corrosive sodium hydroxide, more commonly known as Drano), refined (treated with phosphoric acid, such as is used for washing windows), bleached (with clays, producing rancidity), and deodorized at frying temperatures. What you are left with is a cooking grease with little nutritional value and some toxicity. That's *before* you further damage it by frying and sautéing! The reason I bring this up is that research shows a connection between such oils and cancer, as well as other health problems.

I prefer to use oils that come from organically grown seeds and nuts, pressed simply and without any further processing. They taste like the seeds and nuts they come from and can impart wonderfully rich flavors to the dishes they're paired with, as well as giving your body the nutrients from the source seeds and nuts.

NOTE • Much attention has also been focused on the need for omega 3 and omega 6 fatty acids in the diet. Flaxseed oil is one of the best vegetarian sources of omega 3 fatty acids, but it is poorly balanced, being too low in omega 6 essential fatty acid. It should therefore be balanced with an oil rich in omega 6, such as fresh sunflower oil. As most omega 3 is found in fish, add a teaspoon to salad dressings, but do not use for cooking.

RECOMMENDED COOKING METHODS FOR FRESH OILS • While heating oils directly in the pan damages them, making them unhealthy, oils that are fresh and healthy can be used in cooking with some special care. The best rule of thumb is to add the oils after the cooking is completed, giving you the rich flavor and essential nutrients of the oils.

Question: "How can I sauté without oils?"

Answer: Use just enough water in the pan to keep the vegetables from sticking and the oil from overheating. When oil is combined with liquid, it can not reach more than 212 degrees Fahrenheit, which is boiling temperature at sea level. Another way is to sauté with water alone, adding spices and everything else as you normally would, then add the oils at the end. Both methods keep the oils from becoming damaged and toxic to the body. I've been cooking this way and it's a piece of cake. The dishes come out tasting as good if not better than cooking the old way with low quality oils, in part, because you never get that burnt oil taste.

CHEESE AND EGGS • Cheese often provides a reliable source of protein and amino acids in the vegetarian diet. However, in light of the current emphasis on reducing fat and cholesterol intake, you should be aware of alternatives to the traditional offerings made from cow's milk and their comparative nutritive value. As I am a moderate in most things in life, the recipes in this book call for basic cheeses available at the supermarket, generally used in small amounts. If your diet requires a stricter approach to fat, cholesterol, or dairy intake, the following information should help. We'll use Cheddar cheese as a base for comparison.

CHEDDAR CHEESE (1 OUNCE)

Type	Calories	Protein	Fat	Cholesterol
Cow's milk (whole)	110	7 g	10 g	35 mg
Cow's milk (nonfat)	40	8 g	0	less than 5 mg
Goat's milk (whole)	100	7 g	7 g	25 mg
Soy milk (whole)	70	6 g	5 g	0
Soy milk (nonfat)	40	7 g	0	0

Free-Range Eggs

These eggs are laid by hens that are allowed to move about a yard or hen house freely, as opposed to being raised in tightly packed cages. Free-range chickens are generally fed a diet free of antibiotics and steroids. Read the carton to be sure.

Egg Substitutes

Found next to the eggs in the supermarket, egg substitutes come in pint cartons. Many people believe that this is an egg-free product, but egg substitute is actually made from egg whites. At 30 calories per 1/4 cup serving with no fat, egg substitutes are a wonderful option for cakes, pies, or anything that uses eggs as a binding agent.

BUTTER VS. MARGARINE • To put this argument in better perspective, consider that butter has been around for thousands of years, while the sharp increase in modern degenerative diseases is a product of the 20th century, as is margarine. Butter is a saturated animal fat, containing some cholesterol. For this reason it has been assumed that butter is more detrimental to blood cholesterol levels, particularly low-density lipoproteins (LDL). But newer scientific investigation shows that margarine may actually be more harmful to cardiovascular health than butter.

Margarine was originally made from lard. Since modern margarine production began in the 1930s, margarine has been made from hydrogenated vegetable oils. Hydrogenation is a process by which oils are put under pressure with hydrogen gas at high temperatures to make the oils solid. This process creates a saturated fat that some researchers believe may cause the body to produce more cholesterol than it would from an equal amount of butter. In addition, the hydrogenation process creates high levels of trans fatty acids and other altered fat substances. These altered substances are known to be detrimental to the health because they interfere with normal biochemical processes, many of which have not been adequately studied.

Another consideration: Butter can be used for baking, frying, or heating because its saturated fatty acids remain relatively stable under light, heat, and oxygen. On the other hand, margarine is not good for frying because the unsaturated fatty acids it contains are further damaged by heat, light, and oxygen, and made more toxic.

In the long haul, I tend to go with the more natural of alternatives—butter—simply because we have a better understanding of what it does to the body. Of course, the best alternative of all is to use both of these fats sparingly, and replace them with fresh oils rich in omega 3 and essential fatty acids when possible.

CAUTION: OIL AND WATER DON'T MIX!

Because the methods for cooking with oil in this book are most likely different from what you've previously encountered, there are a couple of tips to keep in mind: First, in all of the recipes that call for sautéing the ingredient in oil and a little water, add the oil and water to the skillet or pot together, before heating the pan. This reduces the risk of being splattered by the water popping in the oil. The other thing to remember is not to allow the pan to become too hot, and not to allow the water to evaporate, as this will damage the oil.

In most of these recipes you can use water to "sauté" the vegetables until soft and add the oil later, if at all.

----

regina's vegetarian table

appetizers

thai garlic dip

baguette avec champignons

guacamole

endive and creamy blue cheese

teriyaki and pineapple cheese spread

green chile salsa

portabello parasols

baba ghanoush

raitziki (cucumber yogurt dip)

silky caesar dip

tomato bruschetta

fiesta egg salad

smoky cheddar pizza bread

asparagus in bondage

thai garlic dip

Makes 3/4 to 1 cup

1/3 cup extra-virgin olive oil

2 tablespoons lemon juice

1 to 2 large cloves fresh garlic,
   minced or pressed

12 to 16 drops of sesame oil

1/4 teaspoon ground cumin

1 tablespoon toasted sesame
   seeds (optional)

1/2 cup finely crumbled, toasted
   bread crumbs

Approximately 1/4 cup water

Salt

The following appetizer has a big punch of flavor, making it a perfect dip for your favorite vegetable. I particularly like it paired with parboiled or lightly steamed broccoli and green beans that have been cooled off to room temperature.

combine first six ingredients. Add bread crumbs and water, stirring until you reach the desired consistency (it should not be too mushy or drippy or it will not stay on dipping vegetable). Salt to taste.

SERVING SUGGESTION • *serve with raw or parboiled vegetables at room temperature.*

IN THE MOOD FOR APPETIZERS • *Appetizers are the prelude to the dining experience, so it's important to set the mood and appetite off right. As a personal preference, I do not like to move on to the main event feeling full, so I tend to serve light appetizers. For example, I might serve the following for a dinner party: Endive and Creamy Blue Cheese (page 7), Tomato Bruschetta (page 15), a small bowl of mixed olives, and a small bowl of fresh walnuts (for those with heartier appetites). A dry or semi-dry white wine would complement all of these appetizers.*

----

baguette avec champignons

Serves 3

1 baguette (or 4 to 6 slices of
    French bread)
Extra-virgin olive oil
2 cups sliced mushrooms
2 tablespoons finely chopped
    fresh basil
Salt and freshly ground black
    pepper
3 ripened tomatoes
1/3 cup grated fresh Parmesan
    cheese

1 cut off a 12-inch piece of baguette and slice it lengthwise. Brush the inside of the bread lightly with olive oil. Put both halves, soft side up, on a baking sheet and bake at 425 degrees F for 7 to 8 minutes—until the outside is getting a bit crunchy, but the inside is still somewhat soft.

2 sauté the mushrooms in a small amount of water over medium-high heat until they begin to soften. While they are cooking, sprinkle the mushrooms with some of the basil, salt, and freshly ground pepper. Remove from heat and set aside in a bowl.

3 slice the tomatoes about 1/4 inch thick. Sprinkle with salt and pepper to taste and remaining fresh basil.

4 while the mushrooms are still warm, but not too hot, toss the Parmesan with the mushrooms and mix to soften the cheese.

5 layer tomatoes on the baguette or bread. Place mushrooms and cheese on top of the tomatoes. Cut into 3-inch lengths and serve.

NOTE • the best cheese choice would be Asiago, but if that is not available to you, use a fresh Parmesan and grate it yourself.

guacamole

Makes 3/4 cup

2 avocados

2 teaspoons lemon juice

1/4 teaspoon chili powder

1/4 cup finely chopped tomato

Salt

The quantity of ingredients may need to be adjusted depending on the size avocado you are using. When possible, use the smaller, darker Hass variety of avocado, which is creamy and rich.

1 remove avocado meat from skin and mash.

2 add all other ingredients and mix until smooth, though some chunkiness is desirable.

SERVING SUGGESTION • *serve with your favorite corn or flour tortilla chips.*

AVOCADOS • *Once called alligator pears because of their shape, color, and rough skin, over 80 percent of the avocado's calories come from fat. Nevertheless, it's appropriate to give the avocado a hearing. The type of fat contained in this velvety fruit is monounsaturated, which has been found to lower cholesterol.*

Because the fat is plant based, avocados contain no cholesterol themselves. Ounce per ounce, avocados contain more potassium than bananas, which is helpful if your body does not tolerate the high amounts of sugar found in bananas.

The only cautionary note, other than the standard concern regarding fat content, is that consumption of large quantities of avocados may cause problems for those taking MAO-inhibitor antidepressants.

----

endive and creamy blue cheese

Chopped hazelnuts

Endive leaves

Creamy blue cheese (Cambazola,
Bavarian blue, or Gorgonzola)

Strawberries or red grapes
(for garnish)

There are times I crave this simple and elegant appetizer as a person might normally crave chocolate or ice cream. The crisp and slightly bitter quality of the endive along with the rich and pungent creamy blue cheese and crunch of toasted hazelnuts tango on the taste buds. Since this appetizer takes only minutes to prepare, spoil yourself with a small portion and a glass of dry champagne.

1 in a 350-degree F oven, toast chopped hazelnuts until light brown, about 5 minutes.

2 cut bottoms off heads of endive and separate the leaves.

3 spread 1/2 to 1 teaspoon of creamy blue cheese into the base of each leaf.

4 arrange leaves in pinwheel pattern on a serving platter with a garnish of strawberries or red grapes at the center and sprinkled around for color.

5 sprinkle toasted hazelnuts over the cheese. Serve at room temperature.

teriyaki and pineapple cheese spread

Makes 1 cup

1 tablespoon sesame seeds

8 ounces Neufchâtel cheese

2 tablespoons Gourmet Teriyaki
  Sauce (page 52)

1/4 cup finely chopped pineapple
  (fresh if possible)

The flavors of the Gourmet Teriyaki Sauce found on page 52 are essential to this simple but exotic cheese dip. Garlic, ginger, and sesame oil are at the base of the sauce. Neufchâtel cheese is used in place of cream cheese to cut down on the fat content (see page 19).

1 toast sesame seeds in a skillet over medium heat, stirring regularly until seeds are golden.

2 mix cheese with teriyaki sauce until smooth. Add pineapple and mix well.

3 transfer into a small serving bowl and sprinkle sesame seeds on top.

SERVING SUGGESTIONS • *use as a spread on thinly sliced bread or crackers, or as a dip for vegetables.*

NOTE • the flavor is best if the dip is used the day it is made.

green chile salsa

Makes 2 1/2 cups

6 to 7 tomatillos, finely chopped
   (approximately 1 1/2 cups)

2 jalapeño peppers

1 small green bell pepper

1/2 large onion (sweet variety)

1 large clove garlic, minced

1 tablespoon extra-virgin olive oil

1/2 teaspoon freshly ground black
   pepper

1 teaspoon freshly ground cumin

1/2 teaspoon salt

Every cook needs a good, fool-proof salsa for today's cuisine. Whether it's used solo as a dip or as a spicing agent in pasta and rice dishes, salsa is rapidly being incorporated in everyday cuisine.

Freshly ground cumin and garlic give this salsa a unique flavor that stands well on its own, or in a recipe. On the heat scale, Green Chile Salsa hits medium.

1 finely chop tomatillos, jalapeños, bell pepper, and onion in a food processor or by hand.

2 add garlic, oil, and spices. Store in airtight container in the refrigerator and use as needed. It should last at least a week.

portabello parasols

Serves 4

1 medium yellow crookneck
    squash (or zucchini), sliced

1/2 cup bread crumbs

1/2 teaspoon rosemary

1/2 teaspoon dried parsley

1/4 teaspoon herbes de Provence

1/2 egg, beaten (or 2 tablespoons
    nonfat egg substitute)

3 tablespoons finely grated
    mizithra cheese (or Parmesan)

1/2 pound portabello mushroom
    caps

1 1/2 tablespoons extra-virgin olive
    oil

1 to 2 cloves garlic, minced or
    pressed

1/3 cup sherry

The meaty brown flesh of portabello mushrooms is becoming a meat substitute in many recipes. In the following appetizer, the large portabello caps create a small bowl that can be filled with just about anything, as mushrooms complement such a wide array of flavors and foods. Here the primary flavors come from herbs, mizithra cheese, and sherry.

This dish can also be served as a light entrée for brunch or dinner.

1 steam sliced squash for 1 to 2 minutes until slightly tender. Chop finely.

2 add bread crumbs, herbs, egg, and cheese to squash and combine. Divide the mixture into enough parts to fill the mushroom caps. Stuff caps with the filling, patting down firmly.

3 heat nonstick skillet over medium heat. Brush pan with olive oil. Place mushrooms in pan stuffing side down and sauté until the stuffing is browned.

4 flip mushrooms over carefully. Add olive oil, garlic, and sherry. Sauté mushrooms until they begin to soften.

SERVING SUGGESTION • *serve hot on top of arranged greens, drizzling any remaining sherry sauce over the top of the stuffing.*

NOTE • add extra sherry at the end of the cooking process to make additional sauce.

MUSHROOMS • *In Oriental medical practices, the mushroom is valued as having many curative powers. They are used to decrease the fat levels in the blood (reduce cholesterol), rid the respiratory system of excess mucus, increase white blood count (boost the immune system), and fight cancerous tumors. The boost to the immune system is thought to be further strengthened when mushrooms are consumed with garlic.*

If you haven't found a favorite variety of mushroom yet, keep on looking—there are about 38,000 species of mushrooms from which to choose.

The only cautionary health note is to watch mushroom consumption if you have gout, as mushrooms are high in purine.

----

baba ghanoush

Makes 2 cups

1 eggplant, about 1 1/2 pounds

2 tablespoons lemon juice

1/2 teaspoon salt

1/4 cup tahini

1 teaspoon freshly ground cumin
    powder

2 cloves garlic, pressed or finely
    minced

This classic Greek appetizer gets its unique and full flavor from tahini, which is ground sesame seeds. Baba Ghanoush can be served as an appetizer or as a light meal when spread inside pita bread, complemented by onions, tomatoes, and any other vegetables of your choice.

1 bake whole eggplant at 350 degrees F for an hour.

2 once the eggplant is cool enough to touch, use your fingers to peel the hardened skin off of the eggplant (the skin should come off easily). Cut the eggplant into a few large pieces and put into a food processor. Pulse until the eggplant is moderately smooth. If you do not use a food processor, mash eggplant with a fork.

3 add remaining ingredients and combine. Serve at room temperature. Refrigerate any remaining dip in an airtight container.

raitziki (cucumber yogurt dip)

Makes 2 1/4 cups

2 cups plain yogurt

1 large cucumber

2 Roma tomatoes, finely chopped

2 tablespoons lemon juice

1/2 teaspoon salt

1/2 teaspoon ground cumin

2 cloves garlic, minced or pressed

This refreshing dip is a cross between tzatziki, a popular Greek salad, and a similar Indian dish, raita. Both are served as a cool complement to hot or spicy dishes. Raitziki and Paratha (pages 208 to 209) make a wonderful light meal together.

1 put the yogurt into a strainer on top of cheesecloth or a paper towel and allow it to drain for a couple of hours. This makes for a thicker, richer dip.

2 peel the cucumber and cut it into quarters. Scoop out the seeds. Shred the cucumber and sprinkle with salt, allowing it to stand for about an hour to remove excess moisture and bitterness.

3 combine all ingredients thoroughly and refrigerate until serving.

SERVING SUGGESTION • *serve with Paratha, flatbread, or sliced crusty French bread.*

silky caesar dip

Makes 1 3/4 cups to 2 cups

10 ounces soft tofu

2 tablespoons lemon juice

2 teaspoons spicy mustard

2 cloves garlic, minced or pressed

1 1/2 teaspoons Worcestershire
   sauce

2 tablespoons olive oil

Freshly ground black pepper

1/2 to 1 teaspoon salt

1/4 cup freshly grated Asiago or
   Parmesan cheese

1/2 teaspoon ground cumin

Tofu replaces sour cream in a dip guaranteed to excite your taste buds with fresh garlic, spicy mustard, and Worcestershire sauce. In addition to reducing fat content, tofu boosts the protein and nutritional value of this dip, while none of its flavor is lost in the translation. This is an excellent dip for those watching their calorie and fat intake (see page 16).

1 drain and rinse tofu. Use a food processor to purée the tofu. Transfer to a mixing bowl.

2 add all remaining ingredients and mix well. Refrigerate until serving.

SERVING SUGGESTION • *serve with French bread slices or flatbread.*

tomato bruschetta

Makes 4 to 6 slices

1 to 2 cloves garlic, minced

Extra-virgin olive oil

4 to 6 slices French or Italian
    bread

2 vine-ripened tomatoes, chopped
    or sliced

Salt and pepper

Splash of balsamic vinegar

Fresh basil leaves

One of the small gifts to surface during the popularity of fresh Italian cuisine is the popularization of crostini. Crostini is sliced, oiled, and baked French or Italian bread. The dish was originally created to use up stale bread. This version, topped with vine-ripened tomatoes, is perhaps the most popular.

1 a d d fresh garlic to olive oil and let sit for 10 minutes. Dip each slice of bread in the oil and garlic to coat lightly on both sides.

2 b a k e at 400 degrees F for 4 to 5 minutes. Remove from oven.

3 d r i z z l e a small amount of olive oil over tomatoes. Sprinkle with salt and freshly ground black pepper. Add splash of vinegar. Arrange tomatoes on top of toast. Top with basil leaves and serve.

V A R I A T I O N • *sliced Buffalo mozzarella cheese can be added on top.*

fiesta egg salad

Makes 1 cup

4 hard-boiled eggs

2 tablespoons finely chopped red
bell pepper

3 tablespoons finely chopped celery

2 small sweet pickles (or dill),
finely chopped

1 1/2 tablespoons finely chopped
onion

3 tablespoons mayonnaise

1 1/2 teaspoons mustard

2 teaspoons pickle juice
(or vinegar)

Dash of cayenne

Pinch of salt

This egg salad has a crunchy texture and lots of color from chopped bits of red bell peppers, celery, and pickles.

p e e l and mash eggs. Add all remaining ingredients and mix thoroughly. Serve in a serving bowl with bread, flatbread, or crackers.

S E R V I N G   S U G G E S T I O N • *serve with unsalted crackers, pumpernickel rounds, or sliced baguette.*

T O F U   V S.   S O U R   C R E A M   V S.   Y O G U R T • *Some considerations when choosing between tofu and sour cream or yogurt: First, tofu is plant based (derived from soybeans) and the others are dairy based. Secondly, tofu is not fat free by nature, contrary to what some may think. Third, tofu is a whole food and does not come in lowfat form (though other tofu products such as tofu cheeses do) while dairy products are available in full fat, lowfat, and nonfat versions. The following table should help:*

CALORIE/FAT RATIOS

	Calories	Fat	Saturated Fat	Cholesterol
Tofu (2 tablespoons) regular	22	1.3 g	0.2 g	0 mg
Sour Cream (2 tablespoons) regular	62	6 g	3.8 g	13 mg
Yogurt (2 tablespoons) regular	17	0.9 g	0.6 g	3.5 mg

----

smoky cheddar pizza bread

12 slices

3/4 cup pizza sauce

1 sweet baguette, sliced lengthwise

Cayenne, pepper, or Italian seasoning (optional)

1 1/2 cups grated smoky Cheddar
 (or half Cheddar and half
 smoked Gouda)

Fresh basil leaves, pepperoni,
 sliced onions, mushrooms,
 olives, or any topping you like

This is a guaranteed party favorite with kids. All you need are a crusty sweet French baguette, some sauce, and smoky Cheddar cheese. The rest is up to you.

1 spread pizza sauce on bread. Sprinkle with your favorite seasonings. Sprinkle grated cheese on bread. Top with any topping.

2 bake at 450 degrees F for 5 for 7 minutes. Slice and serve.

asparagus in bondage

Serves 4

Premade puff pastry, cut into four
  8 × 3-inch rectangles

1/4 cup butter

1 teaspoon lemon juice

1 pound asparagus, washed and
  tough ends removed

8 blades chives

2 tablespoons freshly grated
  Parmesan (optional)

This is a fun dish. Our dinner guests go silly over this whimsical, foolproof side dish or appetizer. Fresh chives are used as the string that ties the asparagus in bundles, but green onion or even packaging string can be used if chives cannot be found.

1 heat oven to 350 degrees F. Bake puff pastry rectangles for about 15 minutes or until golden and puffed.

2 melt butter with lemon juice.

3 steam or boil asparagus until slightly softened. Expose chives to steam or boiling water for a few seconds until they become limp.

4 tie ends of 2 chive blades together and put onto serving plate. Place puff pastry across chive "string." Place 1/4 of asparagus spears on top of each puff pastry rectangle. Tie chives around asparagus and pastry in a bow—the chives are amazingly strong. Drizzle 1 tablespoon paprika butter on top of each portion of asparagus. Sprinkle each serving with 1/2 tablespoon grated Parmesan. Serve hot.

NEUFCHÂTEL VS. CREAM CHEESE • *It's become widely known that Neufchâtel cheese is a lower fat alternative to regular cream cheese. The difference, however, may not be as great as you think. If you are on a fat restricted diet, you may want to substitute both with puréed cottage cheese. The following table demonstrates the differences between the three in calories and fat:*

CALORIE/FAT RATIOS

	Calories	Fat	Saturated Fat
Cream Cheese (1 oz.)	98	9.8 g	6.2 g
Neufchâtel (1 oz.)	73	6.6 g	4.1 g
Cottage Cheese (1/4 cup)			
lowfat	50	1.1 g	0.7 g
creamed	58	2.6 g	1.6 g

salads

broccoli and apple chopped salad

fresh fig and baby spinach salad

caesar salad

banana and cabbage salad

belgian endive with stilton and pine nuts

mexicali corn salad with smoked gouda

old-fashioned bean salad

roasted red potato salad
  with caramelized onions

salade de tomates et l'oignon

pear and sun-dried cherry salad

waldorf pasta salad

yet another taco salad

tuscan bread salad

basil tortellini salad

chinese broccoli and noodle salad

nutty rice salad

cranberry relish

lentil and feta salad with basil

acorn squash and rice

   salad with golden raisins

fresh mushroom salad

asian pear and strawberry salad

mango kasha salad

ensalata per sangue (salad for the blood)

broccoli and apple chopped salad

Serves 4

3 cups broccoli, cut into small
  florets
1 apple, peeled, cored, and
  chopped into approximately 1/2
  inch size pieces
2 to 3 tablespoons sunflower seeds
  (ideally tamari roasted)*
Thai Garlic Dip (page 4) or
  Walnut–Lemon Dressing
  (page 60)

While this may sound like an unlikely duo, my friends and I loved this salad the first time out of the chute. By using the Thai Garlic Dip as the dressing you will get a heavier, more exotic flavor than with the Walnut–Lemon Dressing. The choice is yours.

1 steam or parboil the broccoli until it becomes just slightly tender—do not overcook.

2 combine with apple and sunflower seeds. Add dip or dressing according to your taste, but don't let it become overly saturated and soggy with dressing. If you use the Walnut–Lemon Dressing, you will probably have to add a little salt.

* Tamari roasted sunflower seeds are a good item to have in stock because of their versatility. They have a crunchy texture and salty flavor without the disadvantages of having been roasted in oil.

fresh fig and baby spinach salad

Makes 4 good-size salads

6 to 8 ounces fresh baby spinach,
  washed, dried, and stemmed
8 fresh figs, washed and quartered
Thinly sliced red onion
Grated havarti, fontina, or dofino
  cheese (optional)
Walnut–Lemon Dressing (page 60)
  or Sweet Vinaigrette (page 58)

The challenge with the following recipe is finding fresh figs, which means that you will most likely have to plan on enjoying this delightful salad in the late summer and early fall months.

a s s e m b l e ingredients in order onto a salad plate and serve.

A PARTY OF SALADS • There are times, particularly at the height of the summer growing season, when dinner consists almost entirely of salads. One of my most requested salads is my Mexicali Corn Salad with Smoked Gouda (page 28). Serve this with the Roasted Red Potato Salad with Caramelized Onions (pages 30 to 31) and a crisp green salad to make a filling summer suite of plant based dishes. Add a crusty loaf of French or Italian bread, a fruit juice spritzer or pale beer, and sorbet for dessert and you have a highly flavorful, fresh, and satisfying meal.

----

caesar salad

Serves 4 to 6

DRESSING

1 clove garlic, minced or pressed

1 teaspoon spicy mustard

2 teaspoons wine vinegar

1 1/2 teaspoons fresh lemon juice

1 tablespoon Worcestershire sauce

1 teaspoon shoyu or soy sauce

1/3 cup extra-virgin olive oil or
   other unrefined oil (see Fats
   and Oils, pages xvi to xx)

1 egg, well beaten

Salt and freshly ground black
   pepper

1/4 cup freshly grated Parmesan
   cheese

SALAD

1 small head Romaine lettuce,
   washed and torn into bite-size
   pieces

Croutons (for garnish)

Roman Emperor Augustus Caesar once erected a statue in honor of Romaine lettuce—perhaps the oldest variety of cultivated lettuce—in the belief that it had saved his life. With its abundance of folate and vitamin C, perhaps he was right.

This version of Caesar salad replaces anchovy paste with Worcestershire sauce to create a lighter yet lively flavor. Strict vegetarians should be aware that supermarket Worcestershire sauce contains a small amount of anchovy paste for flavor. Vegetarian versions can be found in health food stores.

1 combine dressing ingredients in order listed, mixing well.

2 drizzle over lettuce. Toss until lettuce is well coated with dressing. Top with croutons and serve.

VARIATION • *bake and slice new potatoes or any creamy variety and toss with this Caesar dressing to make an interesting potato salad.*

banana and cabbage salad

Serves 4

3 1/2 cups shredded cabbage

1 large banana, quartered and
   sliced

1 batch Fruit Salad Dressing
   (page 54)

When I mention this salad to the uninitiated, they furrow their brows trying to imagine how these ingredients could possibly complement one another. All I can say is that while growing up, this was one of the few things in the "green" category that our mother could get us to eat willingly. So if it doesn't work for you adults, try it on your kids. Besides, it's a good way to slip some vitamin C, folate, B-6, and potassium into their little bodies.

toss all ingredients until cabbage is evenly coated. Serve immediately.

LETTUCES • *One of the more noticeable shifts of awareness in fresh foods has been in the area of lettuces. Today up to a half dozen lettuces can be found in most supermarkets, the most common being red leaf, green leaf, romaine, and butter lettuces. Some markets also offer gourmet greens such as arugula, radicchio, endive, dandelion greens, escarole, watercress, and baby greens which have a fuller flavor, often with a bitter finish. The more common broad leaf lettuces tend to be sweeter, but bland in flavor. My preference is to blend the two. For busy lifestyles, pre-packaged, pre-washed, ready-to-eat greens are available in many markets. These bags greens can contain anything from an American blend of iceberg, shredded carrots, and cabbage to an organic European blend of baby greens.*

----

belgian endive with stilton and pine nuts

Serves 4

6 heads endive

1/3 cup toasted pine nuts

3 ounces English Stilton cheese,
  broken into small bits

1/4 cup Sweet Vinaigrette
  (page 58)

It was a happy day when American chefs began creating the blue cheese and nuts genre of salads a few years ago. You can't really go wrong with any combination of these basic ingredients on a bed of fresh greens. In this recipe, pine nuts and balsamic vinegar add a sweet balance to the bitter essence of endive. To dress up the presentation of this otherwise monochromatic dish, use red endive when possible or garnish with a little watercress.

1 remove any damaged leaves from the endive. Cut into 1/4-inch slices.

2 place pine nuts in a small skillet over medium heat. Cook, stirring regularly, until nuts become golden with brown spots. Remove from skillet and cool.

3 add cheese and pine nuts to salad; toss. Drizzle with salad dressing.

NOTE • as an interesting side note, some herbalists believe the slight bitterness of the tender endive leaves stimulates digestive juices as would a dash of bitters in an aperitif.

mexicali corn salad
with smoked gouda

Serves 4

SALAD

2 ears fresh corn

2 tablespoons canned diced green
  chiles

1/3 cup diced red or green bell
  pepper

2/3 cup chopped tomatoes

1/3 cup diced red onion

3 ounces smoked Gouda cheese (or
  smoked sharp Cheddar)

DRESSING

1 tablespoon fresh lemon juice

1 tablespoon rice vinegar

2 tablespoons any unrefined oil (see
  Fats and Oils, pages xvi to xx)

1/2 teaspoon chili powder

Dash of cayenne

3/4 teaspoon salt

When I first came up with this salad I was so pleased that I made it for everyone who came around the house. Sadly, we ate so much of it, it may be a while before we indulge again. Meanwhile, it has become a staple at summer buffets and picnics with my friends and family. Fresh, crispy, sweet summer corn is the key to success with this salad.

1 cut corn kernels off the cob. Add vegetables to corn.

2 cut cheese into small cubes (smaller than 1/2 inch) and add to vegetables.

3 in a separate bowl or jar, combine the dressing ingredients.

4 pour dressing over vegetables and toss until all vegetables are well coated. Serve.

old-fashioned bean salad

Serves 8 to 10

BEAN SALAD

1 cup garbanzo beans

1 cup butter beans

1 cup white beans

2 cups kidney beans

1 cup black beans

2 cups cut green beans

1 medium red onion, finely
   chopped

1/2 bell pepper, finely chopped

MARINADE

1/2 cup rice vinegar (or apple
   cider vinegar)

1/3 cup freshly squeezed orange
   juice

1/3 cup honey

2 cloves garlic, minced or pressed

1/4 cup fresh, unrefined oil (see
   Fats and Oils, pages xvi to xx)

1 teaspoon salt

1 teaspoon freshly ground black
   pepper

This recipe is about as all American as apple pie and baseball. Maybe your grandma used to keep some in the refrigerator. One thing about grandma is that she did not like to waste unnecessary time in the kitchen, as she stood that ground all too often. So this old favorite is right from the can. Considering the variety of beans in the salad, it would be unreasonable to do it any other way.

1 rinse all of the cooked or canned beans and mix together in a bowl. Add onion and bell pepper.

2 mix vinegar, orange juice, and honey until honey is completely dissolved. Add garlic, oil, salt, and pepper, stirring well.

3 pour marinade over bean mixture. Chill for 24 hours. Serve.

NOTE • the marinade will keep the salad fresh for a week or two in an airtight container.

roasted red potato salad with caramelized onions

Serves 8 to 10

SALAD

3 pounds red new potatoes

1 1/2 large onions, sweet variety

1 medium red bell pepper

1 to 2 tablespoons olive oil
(depending on the surface of
your skillet)

DRESSING

1 tablespoon spicy mustard

3 tablespoons white wine vinegar
(or other light variety)

1/4 cup extra-virgin olive oil or
other unrefined oil (see Fats
and Oils, pages xvi to xx)

1/2 teaspoon salt

1/2 teaspoon freshly ground black
pepper

Fresh dill, thyme, or tarragon
(optional)

This simple and elegant alternative to Grandma's potato salad relies on a creamy, quality potato. Use Yukon Gold or Yellow Finn potatoes when available.

1 wash potatoes and cut into small wedges.

2 toss potatoes with a small amount of oil to keep them from drying out during the cooking process.

3 bake potatoes at 350 degrees F for 45 to 50 minutes. Remove from oven.

4 while potatoes are roasting, cut onions in half and into thin slices. Cut bell pepper into thin strips.

5 sauté onions in olive oil and a small amount of water over medium heat until onions are softened. Add bell peppers and continue to cook for another 3 minutes, until peppers are soft, making sure to add water along the way to keep from burning oil. Set aside.

6 mix mustard and vinegar together until well blended. Slowly add 1/4 cup oil, stirring to a smooth consistency. Add salt and pepper.

7 put potatoes, onions, and peppers in a serving bowl. Pour dressing over vegetables and toss until vegetables are well coated. Garnish with fresh herbs if using. Serve.

NOTE • potatoes have nearly twice the potassium found in bananas and are a great source of complex carbohydrates and fiber.

salade de tomates et l'oignon

Serves 4

1 teaspoon spicy mustard

1 tablespoon vinegar

2 tablespoons extra-virgin olive oil

Salt and freshly ground pepper

4 to 5 medium ripe tomatoes, diced

1 small onion, chopped

1 to 2 cloves garlic, minced or pressed

1/4 cup quartered green or black olives (optional)

I was quite surprised when, the first time dining in an average Parisian café, I was served this simple salad. My first question was "Where's the lettuce?" (You can take the girl out of the country. . . .)

In truth, it was one of the worst salads I had ever eaten. Upon being served the salad again at a French friend's home a few days later, I had a change of heart. It's all in the straightforward but tangy dressing. Today, it is one our favorite salads when ripe, sweet summer tomatoes are available.

1 mix mustard and vinegar in a small salad bowl.

2 add oil, salt, and pepper and stir.

3 add tomatoes, onions, garlic, and olives to the bowl with the dressing and mix until coated. Serve.

VARIATION • *add parsley, basil, capers, or anything else you wish.*

pear and sun-dried cherry salad

Serves 2

3 tablespoons almonds, slivered

4 cups mixed greens

1 pear, thinly sliced

2 tablespoons sun-dried cherries

4 teaspoons balsamic vinegar

6 to 8 drops cherry extract

3 tablespoons extra-virgin olive oil
   or unrefined walnut oil

Salt

Freshly ground black pepper

Pears of all types are a very good source of fiber and vitamin C and also contain a good ratio of sodium to potassium. This is a plus in controlling high blood pressure. Sun-dried cherries add a wonderful sweet–tart accent to the salad and can be found in health food stores or natural foods sections of many supermarkets.

1 heat oven to 400 degrees F. Once oven is heated, place slivered almonds on a baking sheet and bake until the almond flesh is a light beige, approximately 5 minutes. Keep a close eye on them as they burn quickly.

2 wash greens and spin or pat dry. Place greens on a salad plate. Arrange pear slices in a pinwheel pattern on greens. Sprinkle with toasted almonds and cherries.

3 in a small cup or bowl, mix remaining ingredients together and drizzle over salad.

waldorf pasta salad

Serves 3 to 4

1 1/3 cups shell pasta

2/3 cup quartered pecans

1 1/2 cups diced apple

2 stalks celery, sliced

1 cup shredded Cheddar cheese

3 to 4 tablespoons Basic
   Vinaigrette (page 57) or bottled
   vinaigrette

1 teaspoon honey

2 teaspoons freshly squeezed
   lemon juice

This combination may sound a little strange, but it makes a nice alternative to the traditional pasta salads at get-togethers. If you are not fond of Cheddar cheese, you can use virtually any of your favorites from pepper Jack to Gorgonzola or even feta.

1 boil pasta until tender, rinse, and set aside.

2 broil pecan quarters for 1 to 2 minutes, keeping a close eye on the nuts so they do not burn.

3 combine all ingredients, except dressing, honey, and lemon juice, and toss.

4 using your favorite vinaigrette as a base, adjust the flavor to a tangier and sweeter dressing by adding the lemon juice and honey. Taste as you go to make sure the lemon isn't overwhelming. Pour over salad and toss. Serve at room temperature.

yet another taco salad

Serves 8

1 head iceberg lettuce, cut up

1/2 onion, diced

2 tomatoes, diced

1 can (16 ounces) ranch-style
   beans (see note)

8 to 10 ounces sharp Cheddar
   cheese, grated

1 small bottle Catalina dressing

Salsa (optional)

2 cups corn chips (thick, crunchy
   Fritos-style), broken up

This is just a basic '70s-era taco salad, yet I have requests for it all the time. It has truly become a party staple for roughly three decades now, and does not appear to be suffering from the ravages of our ever-more-sophisticated culinary tastes. I guess the old reliables are just that for good reason.

1 all ingredients except the chips, dressing, and salsa can be tossed together in advance.

2 add dressing, then salsa, to taste. Add chips just before serving.

NOTE • ranch-style beans are seasoned in a way that enhances the flavor of the salad, making them preferable to plain pintos.

tuscan bread salad

Serves 4 to 6

5 cups cubed French bread

5 cups fresh tomato wedges

1/3 cup fresh basil, torn into
pieces

2/3 cup chopped red onion

1/3 cup chopped green olives

1/3 cup shaved or coarsely grated
Parmesan cheese
(see variation)

1 to 2 cloves garlic, minced or
pressed

3 tablespoons vinegar

1/4 cup extra-virgin olive oil

Cayenne or chile oil

Salt and pepper

There are a couple ways to make this classic Tuscan Bread Salad. The version I made from an English-language Tuscan cookbook I found in Florence calls for baking the bread cubes until they are hard, then soaking them in water for a few minutes until soft, wringing them out gently, and proceeding with the recipe. They were a tad too moist for my taste, but this method does keep the croutons from absorbing all of the dressing and leaving the rest of the salad on the dry side. I have opted for the drier version. Play with it and see what you think.

1 bake the bread at 450 degrees F for 8 to 10 minutes, until lightly golden and firm but not crunchy. Remove from oven.

2 combine tomatoes, basil, onion, olives, and Parmesan in a serving bowl.

3 mix garlic, vinegar, oil, cayenne or chile oil, salt, and pepper to taste in a separate cup. The mixture should be peppery and relatively salty.

4 toss bread cubes in with tomato mixture. Drizzle salad dressing over the mixture, stirring along the way. Toss until well blended.

5 let stand for 30 minutes so the bread can absorb moisture from the tomatoes. Serve at room temperature.

VARIATION • *for variety and increased protein content, add cubes of Buffalo mozzarella, cubes of marinated tofu, or crumbled feta.*

basil tortellini salad

Serves 4

9 ounces fresh cheese tortellini
   (see variation)

2 tablespoons chopped fresh basil

2 tablespoons chopped fresh
   parsley

1/4 cup extra-virgin olive oil or
   other unrefined oil (see Fats and
   Oils, pages xvi to xx)

2 teaspoons lime juice

3 tablespoons vinegar

2/3 cup finely chopped tomatoes

1/2 cup finely chopped yellow or
   red bell pepper

Seasoned salt

Sometimes it's the little things that make the difference. In this recipe, I kept fiddling to find the ingredient that would give it a little extra zing. Voilà—a little seasoned salt did it. Unlike the old days when Lawry's was all there was, today there are many blends of seasoned salt tailored to suit your individual tastes.

1 boil pasta until tender.

2 in a small bowl, combine basil, parsley, and oil. Add lime juice and vinegar. Pour over tomatoes and bell pepper in a bigger bowl and begin adding seasoned salt. It's okay to make the mixture a little on the salty side because the pasta will dilute the saltiness.

3 add pasta, toss, and adjust flavor by adding more seasoned salt if necessary.

VARIATION • *if you really enjoy the taste of basil, you can use a basil–cheese tortellini or agnolotti. If you do not eat cheese, the salad also works with other varieties of pasta.*

chinese broccoli and noodle salad

Serves 4

SALAD

6 ounces rice noodles (or ramen)

2 cups broccoli, cut up

2 bunches fresh spinach (or 1
   package [10 ounces] cleaned
   fresh spinach)

1 cucumber, sliced

4 tangerines or mandarin oranges,
   peeled and sectioned (or 1
   medium can)

1/2 cup peanuts

DRESSING

1/3 cup rice vinegar

1 1/2 tablespoons honey

12 to 16 drops sesame oil

12 to 16 drops chile oil

1/4 cup fresh unrefined oil (see
   Fats and Oils, pages xvi to xx)

Salt

Broccoli, commonly acknowledged as a super food, is the star player in this vegetarian Chinese noodle salad. High in fiber, broccoli is also a good source of vitamin B-6, which is more difficult to find in a vegetarian diet. Broccoli is also rich in calcium and vitamin C. Couple this with all the vitamin A, folate, and potassium in the spinach and you have one healthful, great-tasting salad.

1 boil noodles just until soft; do not overcook. Rinse in cold water.

2 boil or steam broccoli for about 2 minutes, until crisp-tender.

3 clean and trim spinach.

4 to make the dressing, mix all dressing ingredients. You can play with the sesame and chile oils to get the flavor you like. When adding salt, remember that the noodles are bland and the dressing may require more salt than expected.

5 to compose the salad, make a bed of spinach. Layer noodles, then cucumbers, broccoli, tangerines, peanuts, and dressing.

nutty rice salad

Serves 4

1 cup basmati rice (or other
favorite rice)

1 large tomato

1/2 avocado

1/3 cup slivered almonds (or
cashew pieces)

1/3 cup fresh unrefined oil (see
Fats and Oils, pages xvi to xx)

4 tablespoons vinegar

1 teaspoon soy sauce

1/3 cup chopped chives

3/8 teaspoon turmeric

Salt and freshly ground pepper

While we all have our favorite types of rice, I would strongly recommend using basmati rice in the following recipe. Its nutty and delicate flavor makes it queen among rice. While the basmati you find in most stores is from India, many rice growers in the United States are raising it as well. You can use either the brown whole variety or the polished white, depending on your taste and dietary concerns. The turmeric in this recipe gives the dish a subtle flavor and lends a pale yellow color to the rice.

1 cook rice until it reaches desired texture, rinse in cold water, and set aside.

2 while rice is cooking, dice vegetables.

3 place slivered almonds under a broiler for 1 to 2 minutes, keeping a close eye on them so they do not burn. Remove nuts when they are lightly browned.

4 in a small bowl or cup, mix oil, vinegar, and soy sauce. Add chives and spices, adjusting the salt and pepper to taste. The recipe can take a generous portion of pepper.

5 toss all ingredients together and serve at room temperature.

cranberry relish

Serves 8 to 10

1 bag (12 ounces) fresh cranberries, ground in food processor

1 cup walnuts, finely chopped in
 food processor

1 orange (or 2 mandarins), cut up
 and ground in food processor

1/2 to 3/4 cup sugar

This is a holiday favorite and exists in cooking files in many variations. If at all possible, try to find mandarin oranges, which are har-
vested in the late fall and early winter. They have a wonderful
balance of full flavor—tart and sweet. You will need to use two
mandarin oranges to every one navel or Valencia orange as mandarins are small like tangerines.

blend ingredients and refrigerate overnight. Serve.

lentil and feta salad with basil

Serves 5

SALAD

1 cup lentils

1/3 cup chopped red bell pepper

1/3 cup chopped green bell pepper

1 to 2 tablespoons finely chopped
   fresh basil

3 ounces feta cheese, crumbled

DRESSING

1 1/2 tablespoons rice vinegar

1 tablespoon lemon juice

2 tablespoons extra-virgin olive oil
   or other unrefined oil (see Fats
   and Oils, pages xvi to xx)

1/4 teaspoon salt

GARNISH

Lettuce leaves

Tomato slices

The modest little lentil has been used as a nutritional super food in India and the Middle East for thousands of years. Women who are pregnant or taking birth control pills need plenty of folate in their diet, and lentils are loaded with folate. Lentils are also high in protein and fiber as well as a host of vitamins and minerals. In addition to the nutritional value of the lentils, the bell peppers in this salad are loaded with vitamins C and B-6. The feta—lower in fat than most cheeses—adds extra protein.

1 cook lentils in 2 quarts of boiling water until soft but not mushy, about 30 minutes. Rinse.

2 mix lentils in serving bowl with bell peppers, basil, and feta.

3 mix dressing ingredients. Pour over lentil mixture.

4 serve over lettuce leaves and garnish with tomato slices. Sprinkle with a little feta if there is any left over.

acorn squash and rice salad with golden raisins

Serves 4 to 6

1/2 baked acorn squash

1 teaspoon freshly grated ginger

1 clove garlic, minced or pressed

Salt and pepper

1 tablespoon honey, or pure maple syrup

2 cups rice mix (white long grain, wild rice, brown), cooked

3 green onions, finely sliced

3 tablespoons golden raisins

1/4 cup toasted pecans or cashews (optional)

1/4 cup Oriental Dressing (page 59)

Few drops of chile oil

This is a truly hearty, belly-satisfying salad made exotic by the addition of ginger and golden raisins. I like the textures created when you combine a variety of rice. You can make your own blend or use one that is prepackaged. The acorn squash adds fiber and complex carbohydrates as well as vitamins A and C. Nuts, which are optional here, make a complete protein when combined with the wild rice.

1 scoop out pulp and seeds from the half squash. Bake at 350 degrees F for 1 hour 10 minutes, or until tender.

2 cut squash into 1/2-inch cubes.

3 over medium-high heat, sauté squash in nonstick skillet in a little water until squash cubes begin to soften. Add ginger and garlic and continue to cook for a minute or so, making sure not to burn the garlic and ginger, adding more water if necessary. Season with salt and pepper to taste. Remove from heat. Drizzle honey over squash and toss.

4 transfer squash from skillet to serving bowl. Add cooked rice, onions, raisins, and nuts, if using. Toss. Add dressing and chile oil to taste, and stir until well mixed. Serve at room temperature.

fresh mushroom salad

Serves 6

1 pound fresh mushrooms

2 tablespoons extra-virgin olive oil

Juice of 1 lemon

20 fresh basil leaves

1 cup grated Jarlsberg Swiss
  cheese

Kosher salt or coarse sea salt

When we think of nutrient-rich vegetables, mushrooms are not the first to come to mind. Perhaps it's their homely and diminutive appearance. In fact, mushrooms are a respectable source of fiber and complex carbohydrates as well as iron and niacin for healthy red blood cells and riboflavin, which helps keep the memory sharp. Mushrooms also have some potent antiviral, antitumor, and anti-cholesterol properties. Shiitake mushrooms also contain some zinc and vitamin B-6.

1 slice mushrooms very thinly by hand or in food processor; transfer to a medium bowl. Chop basil.

2 drizzle olive oil over mushrooms and mix with hands. Squeeze fresh lemon juice over mushrooms and mix again. Add basil and toss. Add cheese; toss again. Sprinkle with salt to taste, tossing to evenly distribute the salt.

3 serve at room temperature.

asian pear and strawberry salad

Serves 4

SALAD
Romaine lettuce
2 Asian pears, cored and sliced
2 cups strawberries
1 cup blackberries

DRESSING
2 tablespoons lime juice
2 tablespoons honey or pure maple
    syrup (reduce amount if using
    sugar or fructose)
1/4 cup plain yogurt

This pretty, composed summer salad is loaded with quality sources of fiber—pears, Romaine lettuce, and strawberries. Fresh berries should be used for the best flavor and presentation. Any variety of pear can be used if Asian pears are unavailable.

1 wash lettuce leaves and arrange on 4 salad plates.

2 arrange pear slices in a pinwheel pattern on top of lettuce.

3 wash and dry strawberries and blackberries. Arrange strawberries between pear slices. Scatter blackberries over the pear slices.

4 mix dressing ingredients well and drizzle over the composed salads. Serve.

mango kasha salad

Serves 4 to 6

1 cup kasha

2 cups water

1/2 cup diced pineapple

1/2 cup diced mango

1/4 cup finely chopped green onion

2 to 3 tablespoons raisins
   (or currants)

3 tablespoons freshly squeezed
   orange juice

1 tablespoon vinegar, ideally seasoned rice vinegar

2 tablespoons fresh, unrefined oil
   (see Fats and Oils, pages xvi to xx)

1/4 teaspoon salt

Freshly ground black pepper

Cayenne

Dash of nutmeg

Food does not come any more healthful and hearty than kasha. If you haven't already been introduced to this unique blend of grains and seeds, it's time for a new discovery. Made from whole oats, brown rice, whole rye, triticale, hard red winter wheat, buckwheat, barley, and sesame seeds, kasha contains all eight essential amino acids. This is always the most difficult nutritional factor to obtain in a vegetarian diet. In addition, kasha contains complex carbohydrates, lots of fiber, and several essential minerals.

Sold in supermarkets and health food stores with the other grains, kasha comes with a great little cookbook inside the box of a brand name version called Kashi to give baffled new consumers some creative guidance. It is also sold in bulk at many health food stores. In short, kasha can be used in place of rice in most recipes that call for rice.

1 prepare kasha according to package directions by adding 1 cup kasha to 2 cups of boiling water; cover. Reduce heat and simmer for 25 minutes until tender. Because these are whole, hard grains, they will be chewy when fully cooked. Drain.

2 combine pineapple, mango, and green onions. Put the raisins in a small amount of boiling water for 1 to 2 minutes to plump them; drain and add to fruit mixture.

3 in a small bowl or cup, combine orange juice, vinegar, oil, and seasonings. Taste to make certain there is adequate spiciness and salt, as these flavors will be absorbed and diluted by the kasha.

4 in a serving bowl, combine kasha, fruit mixture, and dressing. Serve at room temperature.

WINE SUGGESTION • *serve with a white Riesling or Chenin Blanc.*

SALAD TOPPINGS • *As the salad moves more toward main-dish status, we become increasingly more creative with our toppings. From chopped and toasted hazelnuts to dried cherries and cranberries, the sky's the limit on salad toppings. Most dried fruits will work as well as most varieties of nuts. Here are a few other suggestions: crispy rice noodles, sunflower seeds, chopped green or black olives, and herbed croutons.*

----

ensalata per sangue
(salad for the blood)

Serves 4

2 cups shredded fresh beets

1 clove fresh garlic, pressed or
  finely minced

1/4 cup finely chopped onion
  (sweet variety if available)

3 tablespoons seasoned rice
  vinegar

1 tablespoon freshly grated orange
  zest

Salt and freshly ground black
  pepper

A European friend of mine confided one day that her husband, motivated by distress, runs to the store and buys beets when her PMS begins. This apparently brings back her feeling of well-being. How could this be?

Quite simply, beets are excellent food for the blood, hence the recipe title. Not only are beets loaded with folate, which helps prevent fatigue and depression, they also have a good supply of iron, magnesium, and potassium. These elements strengthen the production of red blood cells and help lower blood pressure.

The onion, garlic, and orange zest help these beets go down easily even for those who ordinarily do not enjoy this hearty red root vegetable.

1 mix all ingredients in a bowl, cover, and refrigerate until ready to serve.

2 serve on a bed of lettuce leaves on a salad plate or in a small side bowl, as the red liquid will migrate around the serving plate.

dressings

gourmet teriyaki sauce

olive dressing

fruit salad dressing

greek dressing

provençal dressing

basic vinaigrette

sweet vinaigrette

oriental dressing

walnut–lemon dressing

gourmet teriyaki sauce

Makes 1 1/4 cups

1 cup shoyu (or soy sauce)

1/3 cup honey

1 1/2 tablespoons sesame seeds

1 tablespoon finely minced onion

2 cloves garlic, minced or pressed

8 to 10 drops sesame oil

3/4 teaspoon finely grated fresh
　　ginger

This sauce was inspired by a commercial teriyaki marinade made by a company called Soy Vay. After having great difficulty finding the delectable sauce, I decided it was time to begin making it from scratch. Honey replaces the sugar found in Soy Vay, and all fresh ingredients are used in this homemade version.

1 stir together shoyu and honey until honey is completely dissolved.

2 in a skillet, toast sesame seeds over medium heat until golden.

3 add all ingredients to shoyu mixture. Refrigerate and use as desired.

NOTE • this sauce lasts for weeks if it's refrigerated.

olive dressing

Makes 1/3 to 1/2 cup

2 tablespoons wine vinegar (or rice
    vinegar)

3 to 4 tablespoons extra-virgin olive
    oil or other unrefined oil (see
    Fats and Oils, pages xvi to xx)

2 green olives, minced

1 teaspoon lemon juice

1 clove garlic, minced (optional)

Salt and freshly ground black
    pepper

Finely minced olives give this dressing a piquant, full flavor.

put all ingredients except salt and pepper into a blender and
pulse for a few seconds to purée the olives. Remove from blender
and season with salt and pepper to taste.

VARIATION • *try olives with a stuffing such as garlic,
pimientos, or jalapeños. If you do not care for sweet dressings, avoid the pimientos as they have a slightly sweet flavor.*

fruit salad dressing

Makes 1/2 to 2/3 cup

2 tablespoons mayonnaise

1/2 cup lowfat yogurt

1 tablespoon honey

1 1/2 teaspoons freshly squeezed
   lemon juice

Lowfat yogurt replaces sour cream for a lighter version of a Waldorf-style dressing that is compatible with any fruit.

mix all ingredients together with a whisk or fork. Pour over fruit and mix until fruit is coated.

VARIATION • *spices or fruit can be added to give this basic dressing a special twist for specific dishes.*

greek dressing

Makes 1/2 cup

1/3 cup yogurt

2 tablespoons crumbled feta
   cheese

1 teaspoon lemon juice

1 tablespoon fresh dill (or 1/2
   teaspoon dried)

Dash of freshly ground black
   pepper

1/8 teaspoon salt

Feta and yogurt give this dressing a rich, cool, and exotic flavor.

m i x all ingredients in blender or food processor for a few
seconds until smooth. Refrigerate.

SALAD OILS •   *As the recipes in this book indicate, I am partial to
unrefined, organic oils not only because of their superior flavor, but because their nutritional
properties are still intact. As for the use of those wonderful nut and seed oils in dressings, as
the French saying goes, "Chaque un à son goût!" ("To each his own!"). Many flavored oils
are available infused with herbs, citrus, or hot peppers. Here are some of my preferences:*

- *Sweet salad dressing: seasoned rice vinegar paired with almond oil.*

- *A slightly nuttier and heavier flavor: walnut oil works well.*

- *Classic French or Italian oil and vinegar: I prefer extra-virgin olive oil.*

----

provençal dressing

Makes 1/2 cup

1 teaspoon mustard (any variety)

3 tablespoons wine vinegar, or
  aged balsamic for a sweeter
  flavor

1 large clove garlic, minced

1/3 cup extra-virgin olive oil

1/4 teaspoon salt

1/8 teaspoon freshly ground black
  pepper

This traditional French dressing is used over tomato and onion salad as well as green salads.

1 mix mustard and vinegar until well blended.

2 add garlic, olive oil, salt, and pepper and whisk until well blended. Refrigerate.

basic vinaigrette

Makes 3/4 cup

3 tablespoons vinegar

2 tablespoons freshly squeezed
lemon juice

1/2 cup extra-virgin olive oil

1/4 teaspoon salt

1/8 teaspoon freshly ground black
pepper

w h i s k vinegar and lemon juice with olive oil. Add salt and pepper. Shake before using. Refrigerate to preserve flavors.

sweet vinaigrette

Makes 1/2 cup

**2 1/2 tablespoons raspberry, blue-
berry, or balsamic vinegar**

**1/3 cup walnut or other unrefined oil
(see Fats and Oils, pages xvi to xx)**

1/4 teaspoon salt

1/4 teaspoon sugar

**1/4 teaspoon freshly ground black
pepper**

Balsamic and fruit vinegars add natural sweetness to dressings for light salads that combine greens and fruit.

mix all ingredients with wire whisk until blended. Refrigerate.

HOMEMADE CROUTONS • *To make your own herbed croutons: Cut leftover bread (French and Italian breads work well) into 1/2- to 1-inch cubes. Heat butter in a skillet or microwave until melted but not browned. Quickly toss bread cubes in butter (you do not need to use much butter) until they are lightly coated. Add your favorite dried or fresh herbs at this time and toss. Bake on a baking sheet at 400 degrees F for approximately 5 minutes, until golden in color.*

For a lowfat option, lightly spray olive oil on the bread cubes instead of tossing the bread in butter. You may want to use a sprinkling of seasoned salt as well.

----

oriental dressing

Makes 1/2 cup

3 tablespoons seasoned rice vine-
    gar (salad dressing variety)

1 1/2 teaspoons shoyu

1/3 cup unrefined peanut oil

6 drops sesame oil

Light and slightly sweet, this dressing is ideal with Chinese noodle and rice salads as well as green salads.

b l e n d all ingredients with wire whisk. Refrigerate.

walnut–lemon dressing

Makes 2/3 cup

2 tablespoons seasoned rice vinegar (the one recommended for
   salads)

2 tablespoons fresh lemon juice

1/8 teaspoon salt

1/8 to 1/4 teaspoon sugar (depending on your taste)

1/2 cup fresh unrefined walnut oil

The following recipe is very light and fresh tasting with a rich base flavor from the unrefined walnut oil. It can be paired with either fruit or vegetable salads.

c o m b i n e all ingredients and shake to blend before serving.

MOLDY (BLUE) CHEESES • *Moldy cheeses are an acquired taste for many, but as with food that requires cultivating a desire, a rich and elegant world of flavor awaits. From the strongest Roquefort to a mild blue Brie, the moldy blue veins give this class of cheese a complex and distinctly earthy flavor.*

To create a blue cheese, uncooked and unpressed curds (generally from cow's milk, although Roquefort is made from sheep's milk) are sprinkled with penicillium glaucum. After the cheese has begun to form, the mass is then perforated with metal needles to aerate the culture, allowing veins to develop throughout the cheese. The cheese is then cured in humid, bacteria-rich cellars. Though this may all sound like a laboratory experiment, it is the classic way dating back to the first recorded mention of Gorgonzola in A.D. 879. The best advice is to begin experimenting to see what your palate can accommodate.

soups

cauliflower rarebit soup

chili soup

savory vegetable noodle soup

peppery mushroom barley soup

orange carrot–curry soup

puréed white bean soup
   with jalapeño salsa

spicy rice soup

madame bovie's borscht

mushroom soup with wild rice

celery chowder

chilled cucumber soup

basic vegetable stock

Makes 1 quart

1 medium onion, sliced

1 stalk celery, sliced

1 cup sliced mushrooms

1 tablespoon extra-virgin olive oil

2 carrots, sliced

1 bay leaf

Fresh herbs (see note)

6 cups water

Many chefs do not understand that wonderful soups can be made without the use of chicken or beef stock. For this reason, vegetarians often have to take the time to make their own soups if they want to enjoy a really good one. Since I find soup to be the ultimate comfort food, this book is heavy on soup recipes.

While this book provides a basic vegetable stock made from scratch, do not hesitate to take shortcuts. If I'm in a hurry, I will often use canned vegetable stock or even vegetable bouillon cubes. Natural varieties can be bought at health food stores including organic broth in aseptic packaging.

To give your vegetable stock a little richer flavor, add a spoonful of extra-virgin olive oil. It's doubtful that any of your dinner guests or family will be able to detect the difference between a vegetable stock and a chicken stock in the following recipes.

1 in a heavy soup pot, sauté onion, celery, and mushrooms in a little water for about 2 minutes. Add remaining ingredients and bring to a boil. Reduce heat and simmer for an hour.

2 strain vegetables out. Add oil. Stock is ready to use, or it can be frozen.

NOTE • you can add any herbs you like—or none at all—to accommodate your own tastes.

chinese eggdrop soup with tofu

Serves 6

2 stalks celery, sliced diagonally

3 slices medium-size onion, rings
   separated

1 large carrot, thinly sliced
   diagonally

3 cups vegetable stock

4 cups water

2 teaspoons soy sauce

8 to 10 drops sesame oil

Salt (or seasoned salt)

1 1/2 tablespoons cornstarch,
   dissolved in 1/4 cup water

1/2 cup tofu, cut into 1/2-inch
   cubes

2 eggs, beaten

What does a vegetarian do during cold and flu season while the rest of the world warms up on chicken noodle soup? How about trying this simple and soothing vegetarian version of that comforting old favorite?

1 boil vegetables in vegetable stock and water until slightly tender; remove onion rings.

2 add soy sauce, sesame oil, and salt or seasoned salt to taste. Stir in cornstarch dissolved in water and continue stirring until broth returns to a boil; add tofu.

3 slowly pour in beaten egg (this part is fun), until all of the egg is set and floating in the soup. Serve hot.

WINE SUGGESTIONS • *serve with a dry Riesling or Chenin Blanc (if you're not "under the weather").*

old-fashioned vegetable soup

Serves 8 to 10

1 large onion, diced

3 carrots, peeled and sliced

2 potatoes, peeled and diced

3 stalks celery, sliced

1/2 head cabbage, chopped

1 can (28 ounces) tomatoes, cut up

1 can (16 ounces) pinto beans

1 can (15 ounces) corn (or 2 fresh
ears, corn cut off cob)

1/4 cup extra-virgin olive oil or
other fresh, unrefined oil (see
Fats and Oils, pages xvi to xx)
(optional)

Pepper

Dash of cayenne (optional)

2 quarts water

Salt

This soup is about as homey and old-fashioned as they come—my mother's vegetable soup. A pot of this belly- and soul-satisfying soup was just the ticket when she couldn't get us to eat vegetables any other way. Near to our hearts, this is truly a comfort food.

1 in a large soup pot, sauté onion in a little water until slightly tender.

2 add remaining ingredients except salt. Simmer for 3 hours uncovered. Salt and oil before serving.

WINE SUGGESTIONS • *serve with a medium-bodied Chardonnay or light red such as a light chianti or Merlot.*

OPTIONS FOR THICKENING SOUP:

When making a tomato-based soup use tomato paste instead of tomato sauce

Sprinkle in bread crumbs until you reach the desired texture

Mashed potatoes can be used as a thickener

Flour or cornstarch dissolved in a little water

Rich cream soups can use evaporated skim milk in the place of cream

Use puréed vegetables such as cauliflower; 1 pound of vegetables makes about 2 cups of purée

----

mediterranean bean and tomato soup

Serves 3

1 cup white beans

4 cups water

2 medium tomatoes, diced

1 to 2 cloves garlic, minced

1 jalapeño pepper, finely chopped

2 cups vegetable stock

2 tablespoons extra-virgin olive oil

1/4 teaspoon ground cinnamon

Salt

Cinnamon and jalapeño peppers give this Mediterranean version of bean soup a unique twist. In addition, white beans are an excellent source of complex carbohydrates as well as thiamin, iron, and folate, which is beneficial to pregnant women.

1 rinse and simmer beans on medium-low heat for 2 to 3 hours until tender in 4 cups lightly salted water.

2 sauté tomatoes, garlic, and jalapeño in a little water until tomatoes are thoroughly cooked.

3 place three-quarters of the beans and remaining bean liquid, along with the tomatoes, in a blender or food processor and purée on a "coarse" setting, stopping before the beans lose all of their texture. You will want some small pieces of beans to remain. Add remaining beans, vegetable stock, oil, and spices, tasting along the way. Heat and serve.

WINE SUGGESTIONS • *serve with a fruity light red such as a youthful Zinfandel or Beaujolais. Or try a full-bodied white wine such as a Sauvignon Blanc.*

mexican soup gratiné

Serves 5

1 large onion, diced

1 cup chopped green bell pepper

1 cup fresh corn

1 cup chopped tomatoes

2/3 cup diced squash (any variety)

1/4 cup diced green chiles

1 tablespoon Worcestershire sauce

1 teaspoon chili powder

Cayenne

Salt

3 cups vegetable stock

3 tablespoons extra-virgin olive oil
  or other unrefined oil (see Fats
  and Oils, pages xvi to xx)
  (optional)

Tortilla chips

4 to 5 ounces (about 1/2 cup)
  Cheddar cheese, grated

Crunchy tortilla chips and melted Cheddar cheese take an old-fashioned vegetable soup south of the border. This is hands down one of my most requested recipes.

1 in a large soup pot, sauté the onion and bell pepper in a little water until onions are transparent. Add corn and tomatoes and continue to sauté for a few minutes. Add squash, green chiles, Worcestershire sauce, and spices to taste and sauté, stirring, for 1 minute. Add vegetable stock and oil and simmer for 10 to 15 minutes.

2 ladle into individual ovenproof bowls. Place 4 to 6 large tortilla chips on top of soup. Sprinkle 1 ounce of grated Cheddar on top of chips. Broil or microwave for about a minute, until cheese is melted, and serve.

WINE SUGGESTION • *serve with your favorite beer or a young Zinfandel.*

asparagus and potato soup

Serves 3

2 medium-size russet potatoes, cut
    into cubes

1 cup vegetable stock

10 ounces fresh asparagus,
    washed and cut into 1/2-inch
    sections

Juice of 1/2 lemon

2/3 cup milk or soy milk

Pinch of white pepper

2 dashes paprika

Dash of cayenne

Salt

This recipe was a solution to the problem of using rich béchamel sauces or cream as the base of asparagus soup. Instead, potato purée is used, which lowers the fat content and imparts all of the potato's nutrients.

1 boil the potatoes until tender. Purée in food processor with half of the vegetable stock.

2 steam asparagus until tender. Remove 1/3 of the asparagus to add later for texture in soup. Purée the remaining asparagus with the remaining stock.

3 combine puréed potatoes and all of the asparagus in a pot and add lemon juice. Add milk gradually to thin the mixture to the desired consistency.

4 begin adding spices, adjusting amounts as you taste. Reheat and serve hot.

WINE SUGGESTIONS • *serve with a Sauvignon Blanc or crisp Chardonnay.*

potato–chili soup

Serves 4

2/3 cup diced onion

1 to 2 cloves garlic, minced

3 large potatoes, skinned and
　cubed

2 cups vegetable stock

1/4 cup canned diced green chiles

Savory salt and pepper

The humble *pomme de terre*, or "apple of the earth," has more than just bulk to offer a recipe. High in iron, potatoes have twice as much potassium as bananas, as much fiber as 1/3 cup oat bran when eaten with the skins, and they are a great source of complex carbohydrates. And their mild flavor—probably one of their greatest assets—allows you to pair them with just about any other vegetable to create a myriad of entrées, soups, and side dishes.

1 sauté onions and garlic in a little water until tender.

2 boil potatoes until they become soft; strain.

3 bring vegetable stock to a boil.

4 in a blender or with a hand mixer set at a low speed, blend all ingredients except 2 tablespoons chiles and 1/2 cup vegetable stock. Check consistency, return to soup pot, and add remaining diced chiles. For desired consistency add vegetable stock. Serve hot.

WINE SUGGESTIONS • *serve with a full-bodied white wine or a slightly chilled, light, fragrant Pinot Noir.*

gazpacho with rice

Serves 6

1 can (46 ounces) V-8 juice (or
   other vegetable cocktail)
1/4 cup diced red bell pepper
1/4 cup diced green bell pepper
1/2 cup diced cucumber
1/2 cup diced celery
1 large tomato, diced
1 small avocado, diced
1 cup basmati or other favorite
   rice, cooked (optional, see note)
3 to 4 tablespoons extra-virgin
   olive oil
Dash of cayenne
Salt and pepper
Savory salt (optional)

Years ago, while anchoring the news at a Sacramento television station, I had the pleasure of interviewing Jeff Smith, the Frugal Gourmet, on a cooking segment. His recipe of the day was a ten-minute gazpacho. His secret was to use V-8 juice as the base, saving the time it would take to create a homemade vegetable base. The result was a spicy, hearty soup that remains one of my favorite gazpacho recipes to this day.

This recipe takes the basics of Smith's recipe and adds a twist or two of my own to make it a light meal in itself. Serve it with flatbread and Baba Ghanoush (page 12) or white bean hummus (page 256, Spicy White Bean Burritos), and you have a great summertime meal.

1 chill vegetable juice. Pour into serving bowl. Add diced vegetables, rice (if using), and olive oil.

2 begin adding spices, adjusting according to your own tastes as you go. (Using savory salt in place of or along with regular salt gives the soup a more complex flavor.) Serve immediately. If the soup sits too long the tomatoes become soggy.

NOTE • basmati rice is native to the Punjab region of India and is particularly sweet and aromatic. In many supermarkets you'll find it in a small box under the brand name Texmati, which is a basmati grown in Texas.

WINE SUGGESTIONS • *serve with your favorite medium-bodied Chardonnay, Sauvignon Blanc, or a light, fresh Italian white wine from Umbria.*

corn chowder

Serves 4

SOUP

1 large potato, diced

1 to 2 tablespoons butter

1/2 green bell pepper, diced

1/2 red bell pepper, diced

1/4 pound mushrooms, sliced

1/2 cup water

3 ears fresh corn

1/3 cup sherry (preferably golden
   sherry)

Dash of cayenne

Dash of white pepper

Salt

WHITE SAUCE

3 to 4 tablespoons butter

1/4 cup toasted garbanzo flour (or
   all-purpose flour; see note)

1 cup condensed nonfat milk

You get a "2-fer" in this one—the lowfat and the "gourmet" versions. It's your choice.

The lowfat version uses garbanzo flour at the base of the sauce for a creamy quality. The advantage of this version is that garbanzo flour, combined with corn and potatoes, creates a quality protein. This is called food combining. A picture of one devotee of food combining, Raquel Welch, is worth a thousand words in demonstrating the advantages of a lifelong commitment to thoughtful eating.

1 in large soup pot, sauté diced potato in butter and a little water over medium heat. Add bell peppers, mushrooms, and water. Continue to sauté until vegetables begin to soften. Cut corn off the cob and add along with sherry and spices. Continue cooking for about 2 minutes until corn is slightly tender. Remove from heat.

2 in a medium saucepan, melt butter (do not burn) for sauce over medium heat. Sprinkle in flour, stirring constantly until bubbly. Slowly pour in nonfat condensed milk continuing to stir with whisk while cooking. Cook until sauce thickens.

3 add sauce to vegetable pot and stir, adding additional water or milk to thin if desired. If you use half-and-half (see variation), simmer until the soup reduces to the desired texture.

VARIATION • *instead of a white sauce, use 1 cup half-and-half. Eliminate step two and just add the half-and-half to step three.*

NOTE • toasted garbanzo flour creates a richer tasting sauce than regular white or wheat flour. It can be found in the flour section at many supermarkets and most health food stores.

WINE SUGGESTIONS • *serve with a young Sauvignon Blanc or light Chardonnay.*

potato soup with leeks and bok choy

Serves 4

3 medium-large potatoes, cubed

2 vegetable bouillon cubes
  (optional)

2 cups chopped leeks

1 1/3 cups chopped bok choy

3/4 cup shredded carrots

1/8 teaspoon ground coriander

Paprika

Cayenne

Freshly ground black pepper

Salt

2 cups lowfat milk or soy milk

James Joyce meets Susie Wong in this marriage of potatoes and bok choy. Leeks create the flavor bond between the two.

Little used in the United States, bok choy is a part of the cauliflower and mustard green, or cruciferous, family. These vegetables are believed to help protect the body against the growth of cancerous cells.

1 boil cubed potatoes in 2 quarts of water with bouillon cubes (if using) until tender but not mushy. Reserve 1 to 2 cups of liquid.

2 while potatoes are boiling, sauté leeks in a little water until lightly browned. Add bok choy and carrots and sauté for 3 to 4 minutes. Begin sprinkling spices a little at a time into the pan with leeks, bok choy, and carrots.

3 reserving 1 1/2 cups potato cubes for texture, purée potatoes with half the milk in a blender or with a hand mixer. Blend or mix only long enough to create a smooth texture without it becoming gluey.

4 return potato purée to the soup pot and add sautéed vegetables and remaining potato cubes. Add remainder of lowfat milk until soup reaches the desired thickness. (More milk can be added for a thinner texture.) Adjust spices, sprinkling and tasting until it suits you.

WINE SUGGESTIONS • *serve with Chardonnay. Even better, try this dish with Johannisberg Riesling or dry Chenin Blanc.*

italian lentil soup

Serves 10 to 12

2 medium onions, diced

4 cloves garlic, chopped or
   pressed

2 quarts water

1/2 cup extra-virgin olive oil

1 large can tomatoes (or 4 to 6
   fresh), cut up

1 pound lentils

Salt

No vegetarian kitchen should be without a good, adaptable lentil soup recipe. Inexpensive and nutritious, lentils are a super food. Found in excavations dating back to the Bronze Age, lentils were one of the first crops cultivated in the Middle and Far East. Perhaps it's because they are plentiful and cheap that they are overlooked in the Western diet. This is a mistake because they are higher in protein than any other legume except soybeans, easily digestible, and rich in calcium, magnesium, potassium, phosphorus, and vitamin A.

The following recipe is a basic Italian treatment and is very tasty and satisfying. To put your own stamp on it, try adding some hot peppers, ginger, curry, or whatever else you like.

sauté onions and garlic in a little water in a large soup pot until soft. Add water, oil, tomatoes, lentils, and salt. Simmer for 2 to 3 hours. Add more water if soup becomes too thick.

VARIATION • *this basic recipe can be dressed up with the addition of curry powder, cayenne, and coriander. This combination of spices will give it a more exotic, Middle Eastern flavor. Another option is to add your favorite fresh vegetables, such as yellow crookneck squash, carrots, or potatoes. This is such an adaptable recipe, you can add just about any vegetable and it will work.*

WINE SUGGESTIONS • *serve with a snappy red Italian Barbera or medium-weight Cabernet Sauvignon.*

USE HERBS AND SPICES TO CREATE YOUR OWN SOUPS • *A thimbleful of knowledge can go a long way for creating your own soups with a few herbs and spices and vegetable and legume combinations. Paired with a good vegetable broth, garlic and onions, and basic seasonings you can usually come up with a good soup:*

Potatoes: *rosemary, thyme, parsley, sage, chives, dill, coriander, caraway*

Carrots: *tarragon, dill, parsley, savory, ginger, cumin, cinnamon, turmeric, curries*

Tomatoes: *basil, thyme, parsley, rosemary, oregano, tarragon, bay leaf, coriander*

Winter Squash: *caraway, turmeric, ginger, cumin, coriander, cinnamon, sage, savory*

Lentils: *parsley, sage, thyme, oregano, mint, savory, cumin, turmeric*

Split Peas: *parsley, thyme, savory, tarragon, caraway, chives, mint*

----

herbed ravioli soup

Serves 4

1/2 green bell pepper, finely
  chopped

1/2 red bell pepper, finely chopped

1/3 cup finely chopped onion

1/3 cup finely chopped celery

1/2 teaspoon chili powder

1/2 teaspoon cumin

1 teaspoon fines herbes (see note)
  or Italian seasoning

Pinch of cayenne (optional)

Pepper

2 tablespoons extra-virgin olive oil

1 1/2 tablespoons flour

4 cups vegetable stock

Salt

8 ounces fresh ravioli (see note)

Finely chopped red bell pepper for
  garnish (optional)

In the days when I wrote for the Food and Wine section of the newspaper and my recipes had a deadline, there were times that I was desperate to turn out something original. But original doesn't always mean better, and often equates to risky combinations of foods.

After turning out an indisputable failure, I was doubly desperate to meet the deadline and, I realize in hindsight, the Great Food Fairy pulled me out of the fire on this one. Suddenly ingredients came dancing out of the cupboard to create a chorus of flavors that ultimately became one of my favorite soup recipes—certainly the one I serve the most often at dinner parties.

1 sauté the bell peppers, onions, and celery in a little water for 3 to 4 minutes, until tender. (Use a food processor for chopping, if you have that option, to create a finely chopped texture, not puréed, that cooks quickly.)

2 add all spices except the salt. Add oil. Sprinkle flour over mixture and stir. Add vegetable stock. Season with salt to taste. You can play with the other herbs and spices at this time, too.

3 add ravioli and simmer for about 15 minutes until tender. Garnish with chopped red bell pepper for added texture and flavor before serving if using.

NOTE • fines herbes can be found at any large grocery store and can be used in many vegetable dishes, soups, and sauces. Be sure to use fresh, not dried, ravioli, which can be found in the refrigerated section of most grocery stores.

WINE SUGGESTIONS • *serve with a fresh, youthful chianti (serve cool!). If you prefer white wine, then serve with a crisp, nonfruity Chardonnay.*

vegetable–white bean soup

Serves 6 to 8

1 1/4 cups white beans, rinsed

1 onion, diced

2 cloves garlic, minced

2 cups vegetable stock

2 to 3 quarts water

2 tomatoes, chopped

3 stalks celery, diced

2 carrots, sliced

3 small squash (zucchini, crookneck, or other variety), sliced

1/2 to 3/4 teaspoon ground cumin
   seed

3/4 teaspoon chili powder

1/4 teaspoon savory salt

Pinch of fines herbes or Italian
   seasoning

Salt and pepper

The subtle, aromatic flavor of this soup comes from the cumin seed. This herb is related to parsley and produces seeds that look and smell like caraway but are stronger in flavor.

Native to the Mediterranean, cumin seeds are available whole or ground. To get the best flavor, I recommend investing in a mortar or coffee grinder and grinding your own spices whenever possible. There's a real difference in the flavor and scent of freshly ground spices and herbs. Mortars are available in cooking and specialty shops as well as some health food stores for $15 and up. You don't need an expensive one to do the job. You can also use a coffee grinder, providing it has no coffee residue inside.

1 soak the beans for at least 2 hours, or overnight, in a bowl containing 3 times the volume of water to beans. (You can elimi-nate this step if you wish.)

2 in a large soup pot, sauté onion and garlic in a little water until tender.

3 add vegetable stock, water, rinsed beans, and all vegetables.

4 begin adding spices, sniffing and tasting to reach a blend that suits your tastes. Simmer over low heat for 3 to 4 hours, or overnight in a slow cooker (Crock-Pot).

WINE SUGGESTIONS • *serve with a young Sauvignon Blanc or Italian white wine.*

BOUQUET GARNI • *French tradition in soup making requires the use of a bouquet garni made from fresh or dried herbs bundled together. The advantage is the subtle infusion of flavors without the textures of all the herbs, leaves, and peppercorns. Bouquet garni are ideal for use in sauces.*

Fresh bouquet garni: *Gather a few sprigs of parsley, bay leaf, 2 sprigs of thyme, celery leaf, and whole peppercorns or allspice. This is all tied together tightly with string.*

For dried sachets: *Cut 4-inch squares of cheesecloth and add equal parts of dried parsley and dried celery to one part thyme plus bay leaves and whole allspice. Tie sachets tightly with a string and store in an airtight canister.*

---

tomato bisque

Serves 4

6 medium-size ripe tomatoes (or
   10 to 12 Roma tomatoes)

1 1/3 cups onion, diced

1 to 2 cloves garlic, chopped

1/4 cup butter

3/4 teaspoon dried oregano leaves
   (or 1 tablespoon fresh)

1/2 teaspoon dried basil leaves (or
   1 tablespoon fresh chopped)

1 teaspoon salt

Freshly ground pepper

1/4 cup flour

1 cup lowfat milk or soy milk

2 to 3 tablespoons grated
   Parmesan (optional, for garnish)

An excellent source of vitamins A and C, tomatoes, members of the nightshade family, were once considered poisonous. It was only a couple hundred years ago that one brave tomato grower stood on the front steps of the county courthouse somewhere in the Eastern United States to hold a public demonstration of tomato eating. The audience held its breath—he lived! Or so the story goes.

Try to use ripe summer tomatoes or fresh Romas for this aromatic bisque.

1 boil tomatoes for about 7 minutes, until skins begin to fall away and tomatoes become soft to the touch. Remove from water and set aside.

2 in a large soup pot, sauté onions and garlic in butter over medium-low heat, making sure not to burn the butter, until onions are soft. Add oregano, basil, salt, and pepper. Sprinkle in flour and stir until mixture is bubbly but not clumped up. Slowly add milk, stirring constantly until you have a thick sauce. Remove from heat.

3 peel tomatoes and remove navel area. Purée tomatoes in food processor for a few seconds leaving some small tomato pieces. *Do not use a blender; this will create unwanted foam.*

4 pour tomato purée into pot with white sauce, stir, heat, adjust spices to your taste, and serve.

WINE SUGGESTIONS • *serve with an Italian white wine such as Pinot Grigio, French Chardonnay (Macon Villages), or other crisp, nonoaky Chardonnay.*

potato and roasted red pepper soup

Serves 4 to 6

1 1/2 whole red peppers, cut in
half lengthwise

5 cups peeled, diced potatoes

1 cup chopped leeks, white parts
only

1/2 cup diced onion

2 to 3 cloves garlic, chopped

2 cups milk or soy milk

Cayenne

Salt and freshly ground pepper

2 tablespoons extra-virgin olive oil
(optional)

Perhaps it was the high levels of vitamin C, which reversed the symptoms of scurvy among the sailors, that impressed the ship's doctor sailing with Columbus. The doctor is said to have alerted the Spanish to the nutritional potential of red bell peppers, which were dubbed "pimienta."

Today, the red bell pepper is most often associated with gourmet cooking—especially roasted red peppers. In this soup the roasted peppers combined with leeks elevate this version of potato soup to the gourmet class.

1 heat oven to 400 degrees F.

2 after removing seeds from the red peppers, rub a thin coat of olive oil on the inside and outside. Bake for 20 minutes. Remove from oven.

3 bring pot of water to a boil and add potatoes. Boil until potatoes begin to soften (do not let them become mushy). Drain off water.

4 sauté leeks in a little water until soft. As they are beginning to soften, add onions and garlic and continue to sauté for a few minutes until the onions soften, adding water if necessary. Remove from heat.

5 place 1 to 2 cups of cooked potatoes in food processor along with leeks, onions, red peppers, and some of the milk. Purée until fairly smooth, allowing some bits and pieces to remain. (A blender may be used in the "chop" mode if you do not have a food processor.) Pour into bowl. Purée the remaining potatoes with the remaining milk, again leaving some texture. If necessary, adjust texture by adding more milk.

6 begin adding spices, tasting as you go. You will find that the recipe can accommodate a generous amount of cayenne and black pepper. Add oil, if desired. Heat and serve. (It can also be served cold.)

WINE SUGGESTIONS • *serve with a full-bodied Sauvignon Blanc or cool light red.*

onion soup gratiné with mushrooms

Serves 4

4 small slices dry French bread

3 1/2 cups sliced onions

2 cloves garlic, chopped

1/2 pound mushrooms, sliced

1 quart vegetable stock or water

1/4 cup brandy, dry sherry, or
   Cognac

2 tablespoons extra-virgin olive oil

Seasoned salt

Salt and freshly ground black
   pepper

4 to 6 ounces Gruyère cheese,
   grated

French onion soup has been a favorite of mine since it first passed through my lips. After becoming a vegetarian, however, I could no longer indulge in the rich, beef bouillon–based delight when dining out. After years of watching longingly as others broke through the crusty layer of Gruyère to the steaming onion broth below, I decided to create my own vegetarian version.

In this recipe, vegetable stock along with sautéed mushrooms and brandy replace the beef broth to create a base you may find more interesting than the old beef version.

1 **bake** or broil French bread slices until firm.

2 **sauté** onions, garlic, and mushrooms in a little water until onions are tender and transparent.

3 **add** stock or water and simmer for about 15 minutes. Add brandy, oil, and spices, being generous with the pepper, and simmer another 5 minutes. Add a little more water if the soup is reducing too much.

4 ladle into ovenproof bowls. Place a slice of French bread on top of each bowl. Cover the top with grated cheese. Place under broiler for about 2 minutes, until cheese is bubbly; remove. Serve immediately.

WINE SUGGESTIONS • *serve with a chilled Beaujolais or full-bodied, nonfruity Chardonnay.*

TYPES OF ONIONS • *The trend in agriculture is toward sweeter and sweeter varieties of both fruits and vegetables. For instance, you can now find varieties of corn that are sweeter than many fruits. This is a logical trend since the sensation of sweetness tends to heighten our enjoyment of other flavors. The same is true in the flavor world of onions. Here are some of the more popular varieties of sweet onions available, depending on season and region: Torpedo, Vidalia, Maui, Walla Walla, and Cipolline (this tiny onion from Italy has a sweet but strong flavor).*

----

cauliflower rarebit soup

Serves 5 to 6

SOUP

6 cups cut-up cauliflower

1 2/3 cups vegetable stock

2 cups water

BÉCHAMEL SAUCE

2 tablespoons butter

3 tablespoons flour

1 1/2 cups lowfat milk or soy milk

2 cups grated sharp Cheddar
  cheese

1 tablespoon Worcestershire sauce

1 tablespoon spicy mustard

1 1/2 teaspoons curry powder

1 teaspoon paprika

2 dashes cayenne

Salt

This has become a standard in our family home at Lake Tahoe. Yellowed and worn, this recipe stays tacked to the bulletin board for those dark, quiet winter nights.

Though a fan of Welsh rarebit, I found it more and more difficult to justify indulging in the classic version in which melted cheese sauce is ladled over white bread. So I incorporated the tastes of rarebit (Cheddar and spices) into a soup to cut down on some of the fat and carbohydrates. In this recipe, the cauliflower has just enough peppery flavor of its own to enhance the Cheddar flavor and carry the spices.

1 boil cauliflower in stock and water until tender.

2 while cauliflower is boiling, begin making béchamel sauce. Heat large saucepan over medium-low heat. Melt butter (do not burn). Sprinkle flour over butter and stir quickly, allowing mixture to bubble a bit. Begin adding milk slowly, whisking the entire time until the mixture turns into a thick, smooth sauce.

3 add grated Cheddar to sauce; stir until melted. Add Worcestershire sauce, mustard, and spices, holding off on the salt until the end.

4 when cauliflower is tender, purée in blender or food processor along with most, but not all, of the liquid it was cooked in. Add puréed cauliflower to sauce. Season with salt to taste. Adjust thickness of soup with remaining cauliflower broth. Heat and serve.

WINE SUGGESTIONS • *serve with a full-bodied Chardonnay or dry white Riesling.*

chili soup

Serves 4 to 6

2/3 cup diced onion

1/3 cup diced canned green chiles

2 cans (16 ounces each) chili
   beans (in sauce)

1/2 cup enchilada sauce

1 1/2 teaspoons chili powder

1 teaspoon sugar

1/4 teaspoon salt

Dash of cinnamon

1 1/2 to 2 cups broth

1 to 2 tablespoons unrefined oil,
   (optional) (see Fats and Oils,
   pages xvi to xx)

A staple of South American cultures for centuries, beans and chiles are an inexpensive way to keep hungry bellies filled and taste buds satisfied. Pinto beans are rich in calcium, potassium, phosphorus, folate, and other nerve-soothing B vitamins. Beans are also a rich source of protein (especially when combined with grains), complex carbohydrates, and cholesterol-lowering soluble fibers. There are few better food sources on the planet.

1 in a large soup pot, sauté the onions in a little water until tender.

2 add diced chiles. Add remaining ingredients and allow to simmer for a few minutes. Serve with favorite chili toppings or alone.

WINE SUGGESTION • *serve with a young, chilled red wine.*

savory vegetable noodle soup

Serves 6

4 cloves garlic, chopped

1 cup chopped green onion

1 quart vegetable stock

1 cup sliced carrots

2/3 cup sliced celery

Juice of 1/2 lemon

1 teaspoon dried dill

1 teaspoon curry powder

Savory salt

Freshly ground black pepper

Dash of cayenne (optional)

2 1/2 cups water

2 tablespoons extra-virgin olive oil
   (optional)

1 1/2 cups pasta (spirals, shells, or
   other variety)

2 cups chopped fresh greens (collard, mustard, bok choy)

Yogurt or sour cream for garnish
   (optional)

Curry powder, lemon juice, dill, and garlic dress up what is basically an old-fashioned vegetable noodle soup.

1 in large soup pot, sauté garlic and onions in a little water for 1 minute. Add all remaining ingredients except pasta and greens. Use savory salt sparingly. Allow to simmer for 10 minutes.

2 add pasta and cook over medium heat for another 10 minutes.

3 add greens and cook another few minutes until the greens have softened and pasta reaches desired texture. Serve hot. (A dollop of yogurt or sour cream can be added for garnish.)

WINE SUGGESTIONS • *serve with a young Sauvignon Blanc or light Chardonnay. A dry Riesling might also be very complementary to the curry and yogurt flavors. Give them a try!*

peppery mushroom barley soup

Serves 4 to 6

4 to 5 cups sliced mushrooms

1/2 teaspoon paprika

1/4 teaspoon chili powder

1/2 teaspoon garlic powder

Dash of cayenne

Freshly ground black pepper

Seasoned salt

1 cup chopped celery

1 cup chopped onion

4 cups water

2 tablespoons extra-virgin olive oil
(optional)

3/4 cup uncooked barley

This is the sort of soup you could imagine feasting on with a hard crust of bread and a goblet of dark wine as an 18th century peasant after a long day in the field or blacksmith's shop. With a full, earthy, and robust taste, its richness comes from the barley.

While much of the barley grown today is relegated for use in the production of bourbon and beer, 6,000 years ago it was so valued that it served as currency for the Sumerians. Barley is still a staple food in Tibet and the Middle East.

1 sauté mushrooms in a little water until tender. Add spices as you sauté mushrooms.

2 add celery and onion and cook for another few minutes, adding a little water to the vegetables if necessary.

3 add water, oil, and barley, and cook over medium heat until barley is tender, approximately 30 minutes. Adjust the salt and serve.

NOTE • to receive the fullest nutritional value, use whole hulled barley.

WINE SUGGESTIONS • *serve with Pinot Noir or juicy Syrah.*

orange carrot–curry soup

Serves 6 to 8

SOUP

4 cups carrots (1 1/4 to 1 1/2
    pounds), peeled and sliced

1 onion, sliced

2 quarts water

2 teaspoons curry powder

Dash of red pepper

Pinch of nutmeg

3 tablespoons sherry

Juice of 1 orange

Salt and pepper

1 tablespoon extra-virgin olive oil

1 rounded tablespoon finely
    chopped orange peel

BÉCHAMEL SAUCE

1/4 cup butter

1/4 cup flour

1 1/2 cups lowfat milk (soy milk is
    preferable)

The secret to the delicate flavor of this popular soup is not the curry, but the quick sautéing of the orange peel, which captures the intensely flavored oil in the peel. This one is a consistent crowd pleaser.

1 boil carrots and onions in water until tender.

2 to prepare béchamel sauce, melt butter in a small pan, sprinkle in flour, and stir until bubbly. Slowly pour in milk, stirring constantly. Continue cooking and stirring until sauce thickens.

3 in a blender, purée boiled vegetables along with some of the water they have been cooking in. It will take two batches in the blender to do the job. *Save the stock.*

4 in a large soup pot, combine the puréed vegetables and béchamel sauce and mix. Add all ingredients except oil and orange peel, tasting along the way for the correct amount of salt. Use remaining vegetable stock to thin soup to desired consistency.

5 quickly heat the tablespoon of oil over medium heat. Do not burn the oil (i.e., smoking). Sauté chopped orange peel until the pieces begin to shrivel a bit and turn slightly beige, about 20 seconds. Add to soup. Reheat soup and serve.

WINE SUGGESTIONS • *serve with a German Riesling, white Riesling, or drier Gewürztraminer.*

puréed white bean soup
with jalapeño salsa

Serves 8

1 pound Great Northern beans (or
    other white beans)

6 cups vegetable stock

2 quarts water

1 large onion, sliced and quartered

2 cloves garlic

Cayenne

Chili powder

Salt (or seasoned salt)

1/3 to 1/2 cup jalapeño salsa

Fresh parsley sprigs (optional)

Crème fraîche (optional)

The Great Northern bean is the king of white beans. Largest in the family, this bean provides as much protein as many dairy products, ounce by ounce, with none of the fat. A half a cup of cooked beans contains 8 grams of protein, only 1 gram of fat, and 118 calories. White beans are also an excellent source of fiber.

1 boil beans in the vegetable stock and water until tender, about 2 hours. If water evaporates too quickly, add more during cooking process, making sure to have enough liquid to cover beans at the end of cooking.

2 in a skillet, sauté onions and garlic in a little water until tender.

3 add onions and garlic to beans. Purée the mixture in a blender, making sure enough liquid is used to make a smooth texture that is not thick or pasty. Additional water may be added to reach desired texture.

4 return puréed bean mixture to pot and begin adding spices, tasting your way to desired flavor. Add jalapeño salsa. Serve hot, using parsley sprigs to decorate the otherwise colorless soup. Since the soup is beige and crème fraîche is white, crème fraîche can also be used in a decorative pattern for color.

WINE SUGGESTIONS • *serve with a light Merlot or Grenache Rouge.*

NOTE • many people avoid beans because of the legendary digestive problems associated with their consumption. Here's a hint that may help, passed on to me by a friend in the health food industry. Place a 2-inch piece of a sea vegetable called kombu in the pot as the beans cook. It is said to reduce the amount of "gas" in the beans. Remove the kombu when you are finished cooking. Of course, you can always soak them overnight.

spicy rice soup

Serves 8 to 10

6 cups vegetable stock (see note)

3 cups water

1 can (15 ounces) crushed
   tomatoes

5 cloves garlic, minced

1 jalapeño pepper, minced

1 onion, chopped

1 carrot, chopped

1 cup rice

1 can (15 ounces) pinto beans,
   drained

1 1/2 cups corn

2 tablespoons green jalapeño salsa

1 tablespoon hot pepper salsa

1/2 teaspoon turmeric

1 teaspoon ground cumin

2 teaspoons chili powder

Salt and pepper

Sour cream or crème fraîche
   (for garnish)

This soup is the creation of the cook at a wonderful bakery called the Queen of Tarts. Unlike many recipes in this book, this one requires a couple of exotic ingredients.

Jamaican pepper sauce and green jalapeño salsa are the flavor base of this soup. If you care to take it a step further, you can grind your own cumin. If you don't have a pestle and mortar, a coffee grinder is a good way to grind spices. The only problem is that an electric grinder grinds the entire seed, whereas using the pestle and mortar you can shake off the hulls and use only the fine powder of the seed. Either way is fine for a soup.

1 in a large soup pot, bring first 7 ingredients to a boil and simmer for 20 to 25 minutes.

2 add remaining ingredients except sour cream and continue cooking for another 25 minutes, until rice is tender. Serve with a dollop of sour cream or crème fraîche swirled into soup.

NOTE • in place of the vegetable stock, 6 cups of water with 6 Herb-Ox vegetable bouillon cubes will work.

WINE SUGGESTIONS • *serve with a Sauvignon Blanc or cool light red.*

madame bovie's borscht

Serves 12 people

2 onions, diced

2 cans (14 1/2 ounces each) string
beets, drained or 4 cups freshly
grated beets

1 fresh turnip, diced

3 carrots, sliced

1 large potato, diced

1 head cabbage, cut or shredded

1 large can tomatoes, cut up

1 bottle (32 ounces) V-8 juice

2 to 3 tablespoons vinegar

1 tablespoon sugar

3 cups water

1/4 cup extra-virgin olive oil

Salt and pepper

1 cup ketchup

Sour cream (for garnish)

Madame Bovie taught me about ballet, romance, the spirit world, and cooking. When she unexpectedly passed away, some magic left the world.

She was a maverick in all things, including cooking. The end result was what mattered, and she did not stand on ceremony where the "means" were concerned. In spite of her formal cooking training at Le Cordon Bleu in Paris, she was not above such stunts as the use of ketchup and V-8 juice to make her borscht the talk of the Russian Orthodox Easter dinner table.

1 in a large soup pot, sauté onions in a little water. Add the other vegetables, making sure to drain the juice from the beets before adding them to the pot.

2 add V-8, vinegar, sugar, water, oil, and salt and pepper to taste.

3 simmer for 4 to 6 hours, or cook overnight in Crock-Pot. This soup picks up flavor as it cooks or sits. About an hour before it is finished cooking, add the ketchup. Serve hot garnished with a spoonful of sour cream.

WINE SUGGESTION • *madame's wine choice: delicious Pinot Noir, of course!*

mushroom soup with wild rice

Serves 6 to 8

SOUP

2/3 cup brown and wild rice blend

1 quart water

1 1/2 pounds mushrooms, sliced

1/3 cup white wine

1/2 teaspoon thyme

1/2 tablespoon dried basil

White and black pepper

Salt

3/4 cup onion, sliced

1 stalk celery, sliced

VEGAN BÉCHAMEL

1/3 cup extra-virgin olive oil

1/2 to 2/3 cup garbanzo flour, or
    white flour

1 1/2 cups soy or rice milk

From the Campbell's canned version served in melmac bowls to cream-laden decadence served in silver tureens at a tiny hideaway in the Netherlands, cream of mushroom soup has always been a favorite of mine.

The following recipe uses something a little different, a vegan béchamel sauce. Toasted garbanzo flour is at its base. Whether making a traditional béchamel sauce or this vegan version, garbanzo flour imparts a much richer flavor than regular white flour. You can find it at health food stores next to the other flours.

1 boil rice according to package directions until tender. Rinse and set aside.

2 put 1 quart water on to boil for the vegetables.

3 sauté mushrooms in a little water. Add 3 tablespoons of the white wine, thyme, basil, white and black pepper, and salt to taste. Continue to sauté until mushrooms soften and plenty of juice has been extracted from the mushrooms. Remove from heat.

4 add onion, celery, and two-thirds of the mushrooms to boiling water, saving the mushroom juice with the remaining mushrooms.

5 when the vegetables are soft, strain vegetables from the water, reserving the water, and put in blender. Add 1 1/2 to 2 cups of the reserved vegetable stock to the vegetables and purée.

6 to make vegan béchamel sauce, heat olive oil over medium heat in a large saucepan. Sprinkle in garbanzo flour, making sure not to let it burn. Stir in milk and continue stirring until sauce thickens. Add puréed vegetables and rice, stir, reheat, and serve. (If the soup is too thick, add a little soy or cow's milk to thin it to the desired texture.)

VARIATION • *if you do not want to make the vegan version of béchamel sauce, replace the oil and soy milk with 1/3 cup butter and 1 1/2 cups milk. Wheat or white flour can be used instead of garbanzo flour as well.*

WINE SUGGESTIONS • *serve with a light Cabernet Sauvignon or Merlot.*

celery chowder

Serves 6 to 8

2 large potatoes, cubed

1/4 cup butter

2 1/2 cups finely chopped celery

2 cups finely sliced leeks

1 cup diced onions

1/4 cup cooking sherry

1 teaspoon fines herbes or herbes
   de Provence

1 to 1 1/2 teaspoons seasoned salt

3 cups vegetable stock

1 1/3 cups half-and-half (or whole
   milk mixed with skimmed
   condensed milk for lower-fat
   version)

Cayenne

If you have ever enjoyed a cream of celery soup, you have to try this recipe. It is a bit on the rich side, with the use of half-and-half, but by the time you divide it into individual servings it is not going to be that damaging to the waistline. This soup is worth the splurge.

1 in large soup pot, sauté potatoes in butter for 5 to 6 minutes, until potatoes begin to soften. Add remaining vegetables, sherry, and spices (except cayenne) and cook for another 10 minutes. Add vegetable stock and cook for another 5 to 10 minutes, or until vegetables are cooked through but not mushy.

2 add half-and-half and continue to cook for about 2 minutes, until the soup reaches the desired consistency. Add cayenne to taste. Serve hot.

WINE SUGGESTION • *serve with a full-flavored Chardonnay.*

chilled cucumber soup

Serves 4

4 medium cucumbers, chilled, peeled, and puréed in a food processor

2/3 cup vegetable stock

1 1/2 cups buttermilk

1/2 cup half-and-half

1 to 2 teaspoons garlic–pepper seasoned salt (see note)

Salt

Sour cream and parsley (for garnish)

There's nothing quite as refreshing as cucumbers in the hot and muggy days of summer. And since we also have so little energy in the heat, you'll be glad to know this cold cucumber soup takes only minutes to prepare.

1 mix all ingredients together in mixing bowl except sour cream and parsley and transfer to serving bowl.

2 garnish with a dollop of sour cream and sprig of parsley.

NOTE • for garlic–pepper seasoned salt, you can make your own combination of spices using salt, cayenne, black pepper, and garlic powder or garlic salt.

WINE SUGGESTIONS • *serve with Sauvignon Blanc or a crisp, light Chardonnay.*

main courses

barley with mushrooms and gruyère

smoked mushroom medley lasagna

pasta with cabbage and pine nuts

new england risotto

stuffed zucchini provençal

greek baked beans and feta

broccoli and potatoes with

   sautéed mushrooms

tomato-basil cream pasta

mushroom pasta provençal

chili sin carne (chili without meat)

spicy pineapple-nut rice

savory cabbage rolls

eggplant lasagna

deep-dish spanakopitta

chili 'choke pasta

spicy broccoli–peanut rice

mexican lasagna

risotto con funghi

chala masala

bavarian potato torte

barbecued eggplant parmigiana

eggplant enchiladas verde

savory eggplant pasta

twice-baked potatoes verde

mushroom stroganoff with linguini

vegetable alecha (stew)

vegetable shepherd's pie

risotto with toasted almonds and currants

cajun red beans and rice

vegetable jambalaya

pasta mediterranee

polenta mexicana

seared marinated vegetables

curried lentils and rice

spinach–feta crêpes

couscous and kidney beans

pomodoro sauce

olive pasta

ratatouille scramble

gumbo stew

pasta primavera with red sauce

caramelized onion and cheddar crêpes

herbed vegetable pot pie

eggplant stir-fry

ranchero risotto

stuffed zucchini

pasta crema aurora

enchiladas verde

zucchini and mushroom melt

barley with mushrooms and gruyère

Serves 4 to 6

1 cup pearled barley

6 cups salted water

2 cloves garlic, minced or pressed

1 cup diced onion

4 cups sliced mushrooms

1/2 cup marsala wine (or cooking
   sherry)

Seasoned salt

Pepper

1/2 cup freshly chopped parsley

2 tablespoons extra-virgin olive oil

1 1/2 cups grated Gruyère cheese

There is something very satisfying and primitive about the feeling of a chewy whole grain, such as barley, between your teeth. This could reflect our ancestral roots, as barley was one of the first cultivated grains. Harvests have been traced back in Asia to 7000 B.C.

Since many of the ingredients originally paired with barley—such as yak butter—can be challenging to locate, we'll keep the ingredients list simple. Just make sure you have a little marsala wine or cooking sherry in the kitchen before you get going. The following hearty combination of barley, cheese, and vegetables serves as a main course or side dish—perfect for a frosty winter evening.

1 boil the barley in salted water for approximately 30 minutes, until barley is tender. Rinse and drain.

2 sauté garlic and onions in a little water until onions begin to soften. Add mushrooms and continue to sauté until mushrooms begin to soften. Add marsala wine and continue cooking until mushrooms are tender and about half of the moisture from the mushrooms and wine has been reduced.

3 season with salt and pepper to taste. Combine barley and parsley with mushroom mixture. Add oil. Next add grated cheese, tossing until well mixed. Serve hot.

WINE SUGGESTIONS • *serve with a young Zinfandel or light Merlot.*

PREVENT "ONION TEARS" • *If you have sensitive eyes and experience eye irritation (or tearing) while cutting onions, try the following:*

- *Keep onions in the refrigerator.*
- *Place onions in the freezer for about 20 minutes before using.*
- *Hold onions under running water while peeling.*
- *Do not cut off the root end until you are almost finished*

---

smoked mushroom medley lasagna

Serves 6

3 layers lasagna noodles (about 3 noodles per layer)

1 pound mixed variety mushrooms

1 large stalk celery, chopped

4 green onions, chopped (including at least 2 inches of the greens)

2 tablespoons butter

1 tablespoon dried parsley (or 1/4 cup fresh chopped)

1 teaspoon herbes de Provence (or Italian seasoning)

2 tablespoons white wine vinegar (or rice vinegar)

1/3 cup vegetable stock

1 cup half-and-half

Salt

8 ounces smoked Gouda, grated

This is one of those dishes I trot out when I know we're going to be feeding friends or family who are accustomed to a meat-based diet. With the rich and smoky aroma of this lasagne, I've never had one guest ask where the meat was on the way out the door.

Try to find more exotic varieties of mushrooms such as shiitake, portabello, or chanterelle. Each variety adds a chewy texture and distinct, subtle flavor to the dish.

1 heat oven to 400 degrees F.

2 cook lasagna noodles until tender. Drain, rinse, and set aside.

3 sauté vegetables in butter and a little water until tender. Add herbs and continue to cook for another minute or so.

4 add vinegar and vegetable stock and cook for 1 minute. Add half-and-half and continue to cook until sauce begins to thicken. Do not overcook as moisture is needed for the lasagna. Season with salt to taste.

5 on the bottom of a 9-inch square baking dish, layer 1/3 of the noodles. Spoon 1/3 of the mushroom mixture on top of noodles. Sprinkle 1/3 of the shredded Gouda and repeat process starting with the lasagna noodles until all ingredients are used up.

6 bake for 25 minutes until heated through. Serve hot.

WINE SUGGESTIONS • *serve with Orvieto, red Soave, soft Pinot Noir, or a light Chardonnay.*

pasta with cabbage and pine nuts

Serves 4

8 ounces wide ribbon noodles

1 small onion, diced

3 cloves garlic, pressed or minced

1/2 head cabbage, core removed
  and cut up

1/4 cup cooking sherry

1/2 teaspoon ground cumin

Seasoned salt

2 tablespoons unrefined peanut oil

1/3 cup pine nuts

Don't judge a dish by its title.

As unusual as the title of this recipe sounds, it surprises virtually everyone who tries it. In the tradition of chow mein, this pasta dish is light, and has great texture and flavor.

1 boil noodles until soft; rinse and drain.

2 sauté onions and garlic in a little water until onions are tender and golden.

3 add cabbage and sherry and continue to sauté until cabbage begins to soften but is not limp.

4 season with cumin and seasoned salt. Toss cooked noodles in with cabbage mixture, and continue cooking for another minute or so until noodles are hot again. Add oil. Top with pine nuts and serve.

WINE SUGGESTIONS • *serve with a white Riesling or Sauvignon Blanc.*

new england risotto

Serves 4 to 6

1 small onion, diced

1 stalk celery, chopped

1 small apple, chopped
   (about 1 cup)

1 1/2 tablespoons butter

1 cup arborio rice

4 cups water

3 tablespoons dry onion soup mix
   (see note)

1 1/2 teaspoons ground rubbed
   sage

Black pepper

2/3 cup smoked Edam cheese or
   other smoked cheese, grated

Risotto, like scones, is another one of those ethnic dishes that American cooks have gotten their hands on and begun playing with. I created this version at Thanksgiving as a way to do something a little different with the traditional flavors. Voilà! A cross between stuffing and Italian risotto. The smoked Edam makes all the difference in this dish.

1 sauté onion, celery, and apple in a little water and butter until soft.

2 add rice and stir. Begin adding water 1 cup at a time. Add dry onion soup mix, sage, and pepper to taste. Cook over medium heat, stirring often, adding more water as it is absorbed, until the rice reaches the desired consistency. Risotto requires constant attention during the cooking process.

3 when the rice is done, stir in cheese until it melts. Serve hot.

NOTE • low-sodium dry soup mixes are available for those on a salt-restricted diet.

WINE SUGGESTIONS • *serve with a light Pinot Noir or Chianti.*

stuffed zucchini provençal

Serves 6

6 medium zucchini

6 green onions, chopped

2 cloves garlic, pressed or minced

8 ounces tempeh

2 tablespoons extra-virgin olive oil
  or other fresh, unrefined oil (see
  Fats and Oils, pages xvi to xx)

1/4 cup water

1/2 teaspoon dried thyme

1/4 to 1/2 teaspoon seasoned salt

Freshly ground black pepper

2/3 cup grated Parmesan or
  Romano cheese

2 egg whites, beaten

1 cup tomato sauce

1/2 cup water

Salt and pepper

You don't know what to do with all those zucchini taking over your garden? Just try giving them away. Better yet, here's a recipe that will take a half a dozen off your hands, and supply you with a very satisfying, lowfat meal. It will also give your body a healthy supply of nonanimal protein.

1 wash and boil whole zucchini for about 7 minutes, until zucchini are somewhat tender but not mushy. Remove from water and set aside.

2 sauté green onion, garlic, and tempeh in olive oil and water until onions are soft. Add thyme, seasoned salt, and pepper to taste and continue cooking for another minute or so until water has been absorbed into the tempeh. Remove from heat.

3 slice zucchini lengthwise and scoop pulp out of zucchini halves with a melon baller or spoon, reserving pulp and leaving a 1/4-inch-thick shell. Chop zucchini pulp well.

4 in a bowl, add Parmesan cheese and beaten egg whites to zucchini pulp. Mix well. Add tempeh mixture to zucchini pulp mixture. Mix well.

5 s c o o p filling mixture into zucchini shells in equal parts. Place zucchini in baking dish or dishes.

6 c o m b i n e tomato sauce, water, and salt and pepper to taste. Pour over zucchini.

7 b a k e at 350 degrees F for 25 minutes.

V A R I A T I O N • *use fresh herbs if you can for an even more aromatic dish.*

W I N E   S U G G E S T I O N S • *serve with a dry rosé or a light Côte du Rhône from the south of France. California also has some delicious dry rosés in the style of the southern French rosés that you might try if you can't find the French variety.*

greek baked beans and feta

Serves 4 to 6

1 cup diced bell pepper

2 cloves garlic, pressed or minced

1 can (6 ounces) tomato paste

1 1/4 cups water

1 1/2 tablespoons packed brown
   sugar

1/2 teaspoon freshly ground black
   pepper

Salt

2 cans (15 ounces each) butter
   beans, drained and rinsed

2 tablespoons extra-virgin olive oil

3 to 4 ounces feta cheese,
   crumbled

The inspiration for this recipe traces back to a beautiful backyard Greek Orthodox Easter dinner. The women in the family each brought a favorite dish to the traditional gathering, one of which was a version of this dish. I was so impressed with the simplicity and richness of this legume dish that I went to an Italian grocery store in the North Beach district of San Francisco to buy dried fava beans to give it a try. Despite tips from the store owner on cooking fava beans, mine were a complete failure.

I went back and bought canned butter beans. Voilà—a foolproof rendition of the Easter favorite.

1 preheat oven to 375 degrees F.

2 sauté bell pepper in a little water over medium heat until tender. Add garlic and sauté for 1 to 2 minutes more. Add tomato paste and water and stir until sauce is smooth. Stir in brown sugar, pepper, and salt to taste. Add butter beans and oil and mix thoroughly.

3 put bean mixture into 4 individual baking dishes, an 8 × 8-inch baking dish, or a 9-inch pie plate. Top with crumbled feta cheese and bake for 15 to 20 minutes. Serve hot.

WINE SUGGESTIONS • *serve with a medium-bodied Chardonnay or Sauvignon Blanc with a rounder herbal character.*

broccoli and potatoes
with sautéed mushrooms

Serves 3 to 4

5 cups diced red potatoes

2 cups chopped broccoli

8 ounces thinly sliced mushrooms

1/4 cup white wine

Salt and pepper

2 to 3 shakes fines herbes (or
Italian seasoning)

2 to 3 tablespoons extra-virgin
olive oil

1/3 cup lowfat milk or soy milk

Dash of cayenne

In this filling dish, sautéed mushrooms take the place of traditionally fattening potato toppings such as butter or sour cream. In
addition to the complex carbohydrates found in potatoes, broccoli
provides a wonderful source of fiber and nutrients.

1 microwave, bake, or boil potatoes until thoroughly
cooked. (It is not necessary to peel the potatoes.) Boil or steam
broccoli, separately, for 6 to 7 minutes. Drain and set aside.

2 sauté mushrooms in a little water over medium heat for
1 to 2 minutes. Add wine, salt and pepper to taste, and fines
herbes. Add oil and continue to sauté until the mushrooms are
tender but plenty of liquid remains in skillet. Remove from heat.

3 put broccoli in blender with milk and purée for a few seconds. (If no blender is available, chop broccoli very fine and add
milk to potatoes.) Add broccoli–milk mixture to potatoes along with
more salt to taste, if necessary, and a dash of cayenne. Mash or
beat until smooth.

4 scoop mashed potatoes onto serving plate or individual
plates. Make a depression in center and spoon mushrooms with
juice into center. Serve immediately.

WINE SUGGESTIONS • *serve with a light
Chardonnay or light Merlot.*

tomato–basil cream pasta

Serves 4

1 cup finely chopped onion

3 cloves garlic, pressed or minced

4 cups chopped vine-ripened
  tomatoes (or canned tomatoes
  in winter)

1/3 cup finely chopped fresh basil

Freshly ground black pepper

Salt

3 tablespoons cream

8 ounces dry pasta, cooked until
  tender

Parmesan cheese, grated (optional)

A little bit of bad is good. That's one opinion anyway, though where food is concerned, some might call it a rationalization. The "bad" in the following recipe is cream. But if you look at the overall picture, only 3 tablespoons of cream are used to turn a basic tomato–basil sauce into a gourmet treat. If fresh, sweet summer tomatoes are available, the cream can be omitted easily for a lighter sauce.

1 sauté the onion and garlic in a little water until onions are soft.

2 add tomatoes, basil, and pepper to taste. Simmer over low heat for 20 to 25 minutes, mostly covered to avoid complete water loss. Adjust salt at the end of cooking and turn the heat back up to medium for a moment while you slowly add the cream. Stir until blended. Add pasta to sauce. Toss until pasta is coated with sauce. Sprinkle with Parmesan. Serve.

WINE SUGGESTIONS • *serve with Orvieto, Soave, or Pinot Grigio.*

CREAM SAUCES WITH TOMATO • *One problem with preparing cream sauces in an acid base—such as tomatoes—is that the cream often breaks up, or curdles. The same can happen when using vinegars or citrus in a cream sauce. One way to avoid this problem is to add a little cornstarch to the cream and continue preparation as directed.*

---

mushroom pasta provençal

Serves 3

1 small onion, finely chopped

1/3 cup chopped fresh parsley

1 to 2 cloves garlic, minced

1 cup finely chopped mushrooms

1 tablespoon balsamic vinegar

Salt

Cayenne

1 tablespoon extra-virgin olive oil

1 to 1 1/2 tablespoons flour

1 cup hot vegetable stock

6 ounces bow-tie pasta

1/4 cup finely chopped red and
yellow bell pepper for garnish
(optional)

The beauty of many French pasta dishes is the freshness of the sauce. Contrary to what we often think, most French sauces are not cream based. Garden-fresh vegetables, from the practice of shopping daily, and fresh herbs are the base of most pasta accompaniments. The following is an example of a highly flavorful yet light and lowfat pasta dish in the Provençal style.

1 sauté onion, parsley, and garlic in a little water over medium heat until onions are soft.

2 add mushrooms and vinegar and continue to sauté until mushrooms are soft. Season to taste with salt and cayenne. Add oil and stir.

3 sprinkle flour over vegetables and stir. Add hot vegetable stock and stir until sauce thickens. Set aside.

4 boil noodles until they reach the desired doneness (see note). Drain and toss with sauce and garnish with red and yellow bell peppers if using. Serve hot.

NOTE • for a little additional flavor, cook the noodles in vegetable stock as well.

WINE SUGGESTIONS • *serve with a southern French red or medium Merlot.*

chili sin carne (chili without meat)

Serves 12

1 large onion

1 bell pepper

1/2 pound fresh mushrooms, sliced

1 can (28 ounces) tomatoes (or 4
   medium fresh tomatoes),
   chopped

1/3 cup any fresh, unrefined oil (see
   Fats and Oils, pages xvi to xx)

1 can (6 ounces) chopped olives

2 cans (27 ounces each) kidney
   beans

3 tablespoons imitation bacon bits

1 to 1 1/2 tablespoons chili powder
   (see note)

1 to 2 teaspoons dried crushed
   thyme

Dash of cayenne (see note)

Salt

Freshly ground black pepper
   (see note)

Did you ever wonder why many people will go for a bowl of chili or a chili dog when stricken with a queasy, "morning after" stomach? It's the chili powder and cayenne. For centuries these two spices have been used as a primary healing agent in the West Indies and South America. Chili powders are said to help improve blood circulation, aid in digestion, and even cure ulcers.

A family favorite, the following chili recipe is one of the few where I still use a bit of meat flavoring. I'm speaking of imitation bacon bits, which can be omitted if their flavor offends.

1 in a large soup pot or saucepan, sauté onion and bell pepper in a little water.

2 add mushrooms and continue sautéing for about 2 minutes. Add the remaining ingredients.

3 simmer over low heat for 3 to 5 hours. (The longer you cook it, the more flavorful it becomes.) Serve hot with your favorite chili toppings. This recipe tastes best the second or third day, so make plenty.

NOTE • with all these seasonings, plus onion and bell pepper, be sure to taste your way through the spicing, waiting until the end to add the cayenne.

WINE SUGGESTIONS • *serve with a chilled Gamay Beaujolais or your favorite beer.*

spicy pineapple–nut rice

Serves 3 to 4

3/4 cup brown and wild rice

1/2 cup slivered almonds

1 can (8 ounces) pineapple tidbits,
    well drained

2 tablespoons unrefined peanut oil
    (see Fats and Oils, pages xvi to xx)

1 1/3 cups shredded carrots

3 tablespoons currants (or raisins)

2 to 2 1/2 tablespoons shoyu (or
    soy sauce; see note)

1 teaspoon curry powder

Generous sprinkling of paprika

Dash of nutmeg

In the Asian healing arts, balance is the cornerstone of health and vitality. This begins with food. Foods are assigned, for lack of a better term, a gender—yin (female) or yang (male). In broad terms, red meats, for example, are yang, while most fruits, honey, and sugars are yin. Everything else falls somewhere in between.

With balance as the path toward perfect health, unpolished brown rice is thought to be the perfect food, falling at the center between yin and yang. It is said to provide sustained energy levels. Other foods that fall into this category are most beans and legumes. The more of these energy-balanced foods we eat, the less we crave sweets and fats. I have found this to be true over years of experimenting with my diet.

1 boil the rice along with slivered almonds according to package directions until tender. Rinse and strain. Set aside.

2 sauté the pineapple in peanut oil and a little water for 3 to 4 minutes. Add carrots and currants and continue to sauté for another 5 minutes over medium heat. Add rice and toss.

3 begin adding seasonings, shoyu first, tasting for saltiness. The amount of shoyu and curry powder can be adjusted to your personal taste. Make sure rice is well mixed. Serve immediately.

NOTE • shoyu is a naturally fermented, rich, mellow soy sauce that can be found at health food stores and many super-markets. It is a little more expensive than the average soy sauce. Once you taste shoyu, you'll never use the cheap stuff again.

WINE SUGGESTIONS • *serve with a chilled Gewürztraminer or Johannisberg Riesling.*

savory cabbage rolls

Serves 6

2 cups vegetable stock

2/3 cup uncooked Kashi (or other rice)

6 large whole cabbage leaves, washed

1 medium onion, chopped

1 stalk celery, chopped

1/2 cup peeled, chopped apple

1/2 teaspoon rubbed, ground sage

1/4 teaspoon dried thyme

Pepper

2 tablespoons extra-virgin olive oil or other unrefined oil (see Fats and Oils, pages xvi to xx)

Savory salt

2 to 3 ounces meatless sausage (optional)

1 egg, beaten

1/4 cup bread crumbs

1 or 2 apples, sliced

At the first hint of cool air, I start digging in the cupboard for sage. For me, it's the final surrender to summer's end. Musky and aromatic, sage gives this cabbage roll recipe its personality. Kashi gives it its nutritional balance.

Kashi is a blend of grains, including rice, wheat, and sesame seeds, that is so well balanced, it makes a complete protein. It also gives more complex flavor to ordinary rice dishes, and Kashi's chewy texture feels good between the teeth. Kashi can be found in the rice section of many supermarkets, but if you cannot find it, use your favorite rice or combination of rice.

1 bring stock to a boil. Add Kashi or rice and cook until water is absorbed. Taste for desired texture and add more water if necessary. Set aside.

2 steam cabbage leaves, taking care that they don't rip. Set aside.

3 sauté the onions, celery, and apple in a little water over medium-high heat for a few minutes, until soft. Add sage, thyme, and a generous amount of pepper.

4 add rice and oil to vegetables, stir, and add savory
salt to taste.

5 microwave meatless sausage patties (if using) until tender. Break into small pieces and add to rice mixture.

6 add egg and bread crumbs. If the mixture is too dry, add 1 to
2 tablespoons of water.

7 place 2 heaping tablespoons of filling mixture in center of
very lightly salted cabbage leaf. Wrap leaf around mixture and
place in baking dish. Repeat until all six leaves are used. Bake at
400 degrees F for 15 minutes, covered, or microwave on high for
about 2 minutes. Serve with sliced apples.

WINE SUGGESTIONS • *serve with a young Pinot
Noir or dry Riesling.*

eggplant lasagna

Serves 8

1 large eggplant, cut into small
cubes

1/4 cup extra-virgin olive oil

1 onion, chopped

2 cloves garlic, minced

1 can (16 ounces) stewed tomatoes
(or equivalent fresh tomatoes),
chopped

1/2 pound fresh mushrooms, sliced

1 can (8 ounces) tomato sauce

1 small can (4 1/2 ounces)
chopped olives

Italian seasoning (or parsley,
oregano, and basil)

Salt

Lasagna noodles

6 to 8 ounces sliced mozzarella,
Monterey Jack, or fontina
cheese, or a combination

1/4 cup Parmesan

Called *aubergine* in French, earlier varieties of eggplant were small, white, and egg shaped—thus the name "eggplant" in English.

While eggplant has been a mainstay of the Mediterranean and Asian diet for centuries, it has been vastly underused in the United States until recently. Because of its neutral, some would say bland flavor, it is an ideal vegetable to pair with your favorite herbs and spices to create a lowfat, low-calorie source of bulk in the diet. In this recipe, the eggplant is so well disguised even the most discerning, vegetable-hating six-year-old would be hard-pressed to identify it in this "meaty" country-style lasagna.

1 heat oven to 350 degrees F. Sprinkle salt over eggplant cubes and let stand for 20 to 30 minutes.

2 heat olive oil and a little water over medium heat. Add onion and garlic and sauté for 2 minutes. (Add tomatoes at this time if using fresh; otherwise wait.)

3 rinse eggplant and add to onions. Continue to sauté for a few minutes. Add mushrooms and continue to sauté until vegetables are soft. Do not let vegetables dry out. Add water if necessary. Add canned tomatoes, tomato sauce, olives, Italian seasoning, and salt and cook over low heat for 25 to 30 minutes.

4 boil lasagna noodles in large pot with a little olive oil until soft. Rinse with cold water to keep them from sticking together. You will need about 3 to 4 lasagna noodles per layer (approximately 3 layers).

5 slice cheese into 1/4-inch slices.

6 lightly oil a 9 × 13-inch baking dish. Arrange a layer of noodles in bottom. Spoon eggplant mixture on noodles and spread evenly. Place cheese slices on top and sprinkle with Parmesan. Repeat layering until ingredients are used up, making sure cheese ends up as top layer.

7 bake for 25 to 35 minutes. Buon appetito!

NOTE • mozzarella has less fat than Jack, but Jack tastes richer.

WINE SUGGESTIONS • *serve with Barbera or a full-bodied Zinfandel.*

deep-dish spanakopitta

Serves 4

2/3 cup chopped onion

1 1/2 cups sliced mushrooms

1 1/2 tablespoons lemon juice

Black pepper

White pepper

Pinch of nutmeg

6 ounces spinach, cleaned and
    torn into smaller pieces

8 ounces mild feta cheese,
    crumbled

1/2 cup ricotta cheese

1 egg, slightly beaten

3 tablespoons butter

8 sheets phyllo dough

A basic spanakopitta recipe consists of feta cheese, spinach, and seasoning wrapped in leaves of phyllo pastry. In Greek restaurants it is served as individual, triangular-shaped pastries, folded like a flag. In my version, mushrooms and ricotta cheese have been added along with some additional spices, making the recipe more suitable for a casserole. This also cuts down on the preparation time.

The real key to success with this dish is the phyllo pastry. This Greek pastry can be found in the frozen food section of the supermarket. The sheets of pastry are paper thin and must be worked with quickly to avoid drying, which causes crumbling. That said, I find phyllo fun to work with, and the sky's the limit for fillings.

1 sauté the onions and mushrooms in a little water until tender, adding lemon juice, black pepper, white pepper, and nutmeg while cooking. Remove from heat and stir in spinach. Add feta, ricotta, and egg, mixing with a spoon.

2 melt butter. Cut 8 phyllo leaves in half. Brush each leaf very lightly with butter, placing one on top of another in a 9-inch square baking dish until half the leaves are used.

3 spoon spinach–cheese mixture onto bottom layer of phyllo. Repeat process of buttering the remaining phyllo leaves and layering them on top of the filling. Trim edges of phyllo to fit the baking dish.

4 bake at 400 degrees F for 25 minutes, or until golden. Serve immediately.

WINE SELECTION • *serve with a crisp, dry Chardonnay.*

chili 'choke pasta

Serves 4 to 5

1/2 pound pasta shells

6 ounces marinated artichoke
  hearts, finely chopped

1 can (4 ounces) diced green
  chiles

1/2 cup sour cream

1/3 cup extra-virgin olive oil

1 cup grated Parmesan cheese

Salt

Some of my friends have chosen this as their favorite pasta dish, and it only takes one look at the ingredients list to see why. It's hard to go wrong with olive oil, sour cream, and artichoke hearts, but small portions are in order as this dish is high in fat. If you are not on a fat-restricted diet, this one is definitely worth trying.

1 cook pasta according to package directions.

2 heat artichoke hearts and chilis in a small amount of water for a minute or so over medium heat. Add sour cream, oil, and Parmesan cheese (see note) and stir until thoroughly blended and heated through. Add salt to taste. Keep warm until pasta is ready.

3 when pasta is ready, drain and toss into chile–artichoke sauce. Serve immediately.

NOTE • if you are grating fresh Parmesan yourself, it's best to wait and add the cheese as you toss the pasta with the sauce.

WINE SELECTION • *serve with an oaky Chardonnay.*

spicy broccoli–peanut rice

Serves 4

1 1/2 cups long-grain brown rice

4 cups cut-up broccoli

1 cup shredded carrots

1/3 cup currants (or raisins)

2/3 cup roasted, unsalted peanuts

3 to 4 tablespoons unrefined
   peanut oil (see Fats and Oils,
   pages xvi to xx)

1 teaspoon turmeric

1/2 teaspoon cardamom

Ginger (fresh or ground)

Dash of cayenne

3 tablespoons shoyu

Salt

Did you know that peanuts are not nuts? They are actually a member of the legume family. While they are a good source of fiber, B vitamins, and magnesium, they are considerably higher in fat and calories than the rest of the legume family. That is why they are best used to complement the other ingredients in a dish rather than eaten alone by the handful. In this recipe, peanuts are used to complement the protein in brown rice.

1 cook rice in boiling water (more than the rice will absorb) for 35 to 45 minutes, until tender. Drain off remaining water and rinse rice in cold water. This keeps the grains from sticking together.

2 when rice has been cooking for approximately 25 minutes, quickly sauté broccoli and carrots in a little water over medium-high heat. As broccoli becomes tender, add currants and continue cooking for a few more moments. Add all other ingredients except salt. Taste before adding salt (more shoyu can be added in the place of salt). Add rinsed and drained rice and stir until the yellow color of the turmeric evenly coats the rice.

WINE SELECTION • *serve with Gewürztraminer, Chenin Blanc, or white Riesling.*

mexican lasagna

Serves 8

1 medium onion, diced

1 green or red bell pepper, diced

1 to 2 tablespoons any unrefined
  oil (see Fats and Oils, pages xvi
  to xx)

1 teaspoon dried oregano leaves
  (or 1 1/2 teaspoons dried marjoram leaves), crumbled

1 can (15 ounces) kidney beans

3/4 cup corn (fresh or canned)

1 can (4 ounces) chopped green
  chiles

1 can (4 1/2 ounces) chopped
  olives

2/3 to 1 cup enchilada sauce

1 teaspoon sugar

Salt and pepper

4 corn tortillas

8 ounces cheese, grated
  (Cheddar, Monterey Jack, or
  both; see note)

This Mexican version of lasagna offers a wide range of nutrients, including protein and fiber. The most distinctive flavor in this dish comes from oregano. Oregano is a member of the mint family, as is basil, and comes in a variety of strengths and flavors. Oregano can be easily substituted with marjoram.

1 in a large saucepan, sauté onion and bell pepper in oil and enough water to keep vegetables from drying out over medium heat for 2 to 3 minutes, or until they just begin to soften. Add oregano and stir.

2 add beans, corn, chiles, olives, enchilada sauce, sugar, and salt and pepper to taste.

3 put 2 tortillas on the bottom of an 8 × 11-inch baking dish. Spoon half the vegetable mixture over the tortillas. Sprinkle half the grated cheese over the vegetables. Repeat the process with 2 more tortillas, vegetables, and cheese.

4 bake at 375 degrees F for about 25 minutes until heated through. Serve immediately.

NOTE • if you enjoy the cheese but don't want the fat and cholesterol, this would be a good recipe to experiment with soy-based cheeses. They can be used in place of, or along with, the dairy version.

WINE SUGGESTIONS • *serve with a light Cabernet Sauvignon or your favorite beer.*

risotto con funghi

Serves 6

MUSHROOMS

1 1/2 pounds mushrooms, sliced

3 tablespoons butter

1/4 cup wine

2 to 3 cloves garlic, pressed or
    finely minced

Savory salt and pepper

RISOTTO

1 cup chopped onion

3 tablespoons extra-virgin olive oil

2 cups arborio rice

3 cups vegetable stock

1 cup Champagne (or dry white
    wine)

1 cup water

Savory salt and pepper

1 cup grated Parmigiano-Reggiano

A staple of northern Italian cuisine, risotto is used much as southern Italy uses pasta. It is served virtually every day in one guise or another. What distinguishes risotto, or arborio rice, from any of the thousands of other varieties of rice, is the creamy texture after cooking. Part of the creaminess comes from the preparation of risotto in which small amounts of liquid are added throughout the cooking process until the rice reaches the desired texture.

Champagne or dry white wine and a true Parmigiano-Reggiano cheese are what give this classic version of risotto its flavor.

1 sauté sliced mushrooms in butter and 1/4 cup wine until tender. Season with garlic, savory salt, and pepper while cooking. Remove from heat once mushrooms become limp but a large amount of liquid remains.

2 to make risotto, sauté onions in olive oil and a little water until tender. Add rice to onions and stir.

3 combine vegetable stock, Champagne, and water to make 5 cups of liquid. Heat in saucepan until just under the boiling point. Begin adding liquid, 1 cup at a time, to the rice, stirring constantly. Continue adding liquid and stirring until rice reaches the desired texture, adding savory salt and pepper along the way. When risotto is done, stir in grated Parmigiano-Reggiano.

4 quickly reheat mushrooms and mushroom juice. Spoon over individual portions of risotto and serve.

WINE SUGGESTIONS • *serve with Chianti or Italian Barbera.*

chala masala

Serves 4 to 5

1 pound dry garbanzo beans (or 2 cans cooked, 16 ounces each)

1 cup rice

1 tablespoon any unrefined oil, or butter (see Fats and Oils, pages xvi to xx)

1/4 teaspoon salt

1 large onion, diced

1 large tomato, diced

3 to 4 cloves garlic, crushed

Ginger (fresh preferred)

3 tablespoons extra-virgin olive oil

1 teaspoon garam masala (see note)

Cayenne

Salt and pepper

1/2 cup tomato sauce

1/2 teaspoon baking soda

1 1/2 cups water

Raisins (optional)

I learned most of the Indian recipes in this book from the Dhinsa family of Modesto, California. My friendship with their daughter Monica eventually took us to their home for a cooking lesson after a decade of oohing and ahhing over her mother's traditional Indian cooking. This food is so satisfying and healthful that I now find myself craving it when I am stressed out or depleted in energy.

The basic ingredient in Chala Masala is garbanzo beans, or chick-peas, as they're also called. They are a higher-than-average source of fiber and a good source of complex carbohydrates. Chick-peas also get high marks for containing immunity-boosting folate, B-6, and iron.

1 soak garbanzos overnight (if using dry), drain off liquid, and boil for approximately 45 minutes until tender.

2 while preparing sauce, boil rice with oil and salt to desired doneness.

3 in a large saucepan, sauté onion, tomato, garlic, and ginger in 3 tablespoons olive oil and enough water to keep vegetables from drying out and sticking. Stir well. Continue to sauté, adding garam masala, cayenne, salt, pepper, and tomato sauce, stirring well. Finally, add baking soda, garbanzos, and water.

4 simmer for 20 to 30 minutes until onions and tomatoes are very soft. For an interesting twist, add raisins to mixture during the last few minutes of cooking. Serve over rice.

NOTE • garam masala is an Indian spice mixture that can be found in Indian, import, or gourmet shops.

WINE SUGGESTIONS • *serve with a spicy Gewürztraminer or fragrant Chenin Blanc.*

bavarian potato torte

Serves 4

1/2 pound fresh mushrooms, sliced

1/3 cup finely chopped celery

2 large cloves garlic, finely minced
 or pressed

1/3 to 1/2 cup chopped green
 onions

Dash of white pepper

Salt and black pepper

1/2 lemon

2 to 3 tablespoons extra-virgin
 olive oil

4 medium red potatoes, thinly
 sliced lengthwise

1 1/2 cups grated Gouda

Dill

1 large tomato, thinly sliced

Bavarians know their potatoes. Between *Kartoffelsalat* (potato salad), *Kartoffelpuffer* (potato pancakes), *Kartoffelknoedel* (potato dumplings), and *pommes frites* (French fries), potatoes are a vegetarian's primary sustenance on visits to Bavaria. There's little else for a vegetarian to eat in this beautiful, Disneyesque part of the world.

This recipe was inspired by a dish at a little, out-of-the-way café in the Bavarian countryside that served a scalloped potato dish layered with spinach. I replaced the spinach with mushrooms, but you may want to add it back in as a healthful variation.

1 sauté mushrooms, celery, garlic, and onions in a little water until tender. Add dash of white pepper, salt, black pepper, and some lemon juice to vegetables while they are cooking. Add oil and remove from heat.

2 place a layer of sliced potatoes on the bottom of 9-inch square baking dish. Place half of mushroom mixture on top of potatoes. Sprinkle with one-third of cheese. Add another layer of potatoes. Brush with garlic–olive oil; sprinkle on a little lemon juice, salt, black pepper, and dill. Add a layer of tomato slices. Add another layer of potato, brush with garlic–olive oil, and sprinkle with lemon juice and seasonings. Add the remaining mushroom mixture. Sprinkle with another portion of cheese. Repeat potato, garlic–olive oil, and so on. Top with remaining cheese.

3 bake at 350 degrees F for 1 hour and 15 minutes, until potatoes are tender in the center.

WINE SUGGESTIONS • *serve with light- or medium-bodied Chardonnay, dry German Riesling, or Alsatian Pinot Grigio.*

barbecued eggplant parmigiana

Serves 6 to 8

1 large eggplant, cut into 1/4-inch
   slices

Olive oil

Pepper

1 small bottle (14 ounces) quality
   marinara sauce (or Pomodoro
   Sauce, pages 166 to 167)

12 ounces fontina cheese, thinly
   sliced (see note)

Parmesan cheese, grated

One of the loneliest experiences a vegetarian faces is watching everyone else anxiously waiting for dinner around the barbecue. Take heart. This smoky version of eggplant parmigiana puts non-meat eaters at a barbecue right in the center of the party scene. In fact, you'd better make plenty, because hot dogs and hamburgers pale next to this dish. I witnessed this while serving it to a group of firefighters at a backyard party. Gone in a gulp!

The premade sauce allows you to put this together in minutes. Use any of the spicy variations for added zest.

1 salt eggplant slices on each side. Allow to sit for 20 minutes and rinse.

2 prepare coals in the barbecue. Rub or brush a small amount of olive oil on each slice of eggplant slices to keep them from sticking to grill and sprinkle with pepper. Arrange on barbecue and grill both sides until eggplant is limp but not mushy.

3 place eggplant slices on a metal cookie sheet so each one is slightly overlapping its neighbor. Spoon marinara sauce over the eggplant slices until they are covered. Place sliced fontina on top of eggplant and sprinkle with Parmesan. Put cookie sheet on barbecue, cover, and cook until cheese is melted. To get a bubbly, browned texture, put under kitchen broiler for about a minute before serving.

NOTE • you may have to go to a deli or gourmet store to find an Italian fontina, but the flavor is worth it. Monterey Jack or mozzarella can be used as a substitute, but they will not have as complex and rich a flavor.

WINE SUGGESTIONS • *serve with a youthful, light chianti or Valpolicella. If you prefer white wine, then try an Italian white such as Orvieto or Gavi.*

eggplant enchiladas verde

Serves 8

1 large eggplant, peeled and cut
    into thin strips

1 large white onion, sliced or diced

1 small green chile, finely chopped

Seasoned salt

1 can (8 ounces) corn, drained (or
    2 ears corn, cut from the cob)

1 can (32 ounces) green chile
    enchilada sauce

1 cup vegetable stock

1 tablespoon cornstarch

8 large corn tortillas

8 ounces Monterey Jack cheese,
    grated

Many people avoid cheese because of its high fat content. It is important to keep in mind, however, that if your diet is primarily vegetarian, most of what you eat is naturally low in fat and cholesterol. This allows for occasional indiscretions, such as pizza, ice cream, or Eggplant Enchiladas Verde.

A factor working in cheese's favor is vitamin B-12. For some inexplicable reason, B-12 produced in the vegetable kingdom, such as that found in certain sea vegetables, is not assimilated by the human body. Animal sources of B-12, such as dairy and eggs, are assimilated. Vitamin B-12 is critical for healthy functioning of the nervous system.

1 salt eggplant strips and set aside. Sauté onion in a little water until tender. Rinse salt from eggplant. Add eggplant to onions, along with enough water to keep eggplant from sticking, and continue to sauté until eggplant is tender but not mushy. Add green chile and cook for another minute or so. Sprinkle with seasoned salt. Add corn, stir, and remove from heat.

2 in a saucepan, combine enchilada sauce and vegetable stock. Heat until the mixture is just beginning to boil. Mix cornstarch with 1 to 2 tablespoons water or stock until all lumps are dissolved. Add the cornstarch to the enchilada sauce and stir until sauce begins to thicken.

3 pour some of the enchilada sauce in the bottom of a large baking dish. Spoon eggplant filling into corn tortillas and roll them up, placing the loose edges face down in the baking dish. Pour the remainder of the sauce over enchiladas. Top with grated cheese and bake at 350 degrees F for 25 minutes. Serve hot as is, or garnish with olives, sour cream, guacamole, or other topping.

WINE SUGGESTIONS • *serve with a fruity Sauvignon Blanc or youthful Zinfandel.*

savory eggplant pasta

Serves 4 to 6

6 to 8 ounces pasta (fettuccine
   preferred)

2 stalks celery, sliced

1 cup onion, sliced

2 bay leaves

6 whole cloves

2 red or green bell peppers, sliced

4 cups skinned and finely diced
   eggplant

1 teaspoon basil

Paprika

Salt and pepper

1/3 cup extra-virgin olive oil

If you spread this distinctly Mediterranean eggplant mixture on bread or crackers, it would be called Poor Man's Caviar or Eggplant Caviar. Toss it in with fettuccine and you have a unique entrée.

The richness or caviar-like quality of this dish relies on the liberal use of olive oil. In light of the concern about oils in the diet, there are a few things to keep in mind. Fresh, unrefined oils, including extra-virgin olive oil, contain some essential components for good health (see Fats and Oils, pages xvi to xx). The key is to use them wisely—don't overheat oils, as overheating destroys the healthful benefits of the oil and creates unhealthy toxins. Olive oil has received the lion's share of attention because of its pervasive use in the Mediterranean. In these countries the oil is often added after the cooking is completed, and, perhaps not coincidentally, the rates of coronary disease are typically low.

1 boil pasta until it reaches desired doneness; drain and rinse in cold water.

2 boil celery, onion, bay leaves, and cloves in a quart of water for about 5 minutes. Add bell pepper and continue to boil until vegetables are tender. Strain, removing bay leaves and cloves.

3 sauté eggplant in water (enough to keep the eggplant from sticking or burning) until tender.

4 grind boiled vegetables in food processor or blender until you have a coarsely ground pulp.

5 add ground vegetables and basil to eggplant and cook over medium-high heat until the moisture from the vegetables reduces. Add generous sprinklings of paprika, salt, and pepper. Continue cooking for a couple more minutes. Add oil. Toss cooked pasta into mixture until thoroughly coated. Serve immediately.

WINE SELECTION • *serve with a full-bodied white, Chardonnay, oaky Sauvignon Blanc, or flavorful Merlot.*

twice-baked potatoes verde

Serves 4 to 8

4 large russet potatoes

2 cups chopped broccoli

2/3 cup lowfat milk

1 bottle (8 ounces) green taco
   sauce

8 ounces Cheddar cheese, grated

Salt and pepper

Cayenne (optional)

As a little guy, Stuart Campbell would have told you that "green potatoes" were the best thing his mom makes. I told him they were green because I dyed them for St. Patty's Day, which is when I created this dish.

The reason to keep the source of this dish's color a secret from kids is that the potatoes are tinted with puréed broccoli. By the time you pour in the taco sauce and add a little Cheddar cheese, the broccoli is just a source of nutrients, only slightly identifiable in the overall flavor.

In addition, the combination of potatoes, broccoli, and cheese make a nutritionally well rounded dish that can be frozen and reheated in the microwave for a healthful and belly-satisfying quick meal. This dish is truly a family favorite for both flavor and convenience.

1 wash the potatoes and dry with a towel. With your fingers, rub a small amount of oil on the skins to keep them from drying out during baking. Bake at 400 degrees F for 15 minutes. Pierce the potatoes a couple of times with a fork. Reduce temperature to 350 degrees F and continue baking for another 45 minutes, or until the potatoes are tender when poked or pinched. (They can be baked a day or two in advance if it's more convenient. They can also be cooked in the microwave. Be sure to oil and pierce the skins before microwaving.)

2 while the potatoes are baking, steam or boil the broccoli until tender. Put the broccoli, along with half of the milk, in a blender or food processor and purée.

3 slice the potatoes in half and scoop out the contents into a mixing bowl, leaving a fairly thin jacket. Arrange the potato jackets on a baking sheet.

4 add broccoli and all the remaining ingredients to the potato pulp and mix by hand or with an electric mixer. Adjust the texture of the potatoes to your liking by using more or less milk, though you don't want them to be too thin and runny.

5 spoon a generous amount of the filling into the jackets. Bake at 350 degrees F for 15 to 20 minutes. Serve immediately.

WINE SUGGESTIONS • *serve with a soft red served cool or Pinot Noir.*

mushroom stroganoff with linguini

Serves 4

6 ounces linguini

1 1/4 pounds mushrooms, sliced

1/2 teaspoon dried thyme leaves

Dash of white pepper

Seasoned salt

Black pepper

1 cup lowfat or regular sour cream

1 cup vegetable stock

2 tablespoons warm water

2 tablespoons flour

Grated Parmesan (for garnish)

The world's forests produce about 38,000 species of mushrooms, longtime companions of the gourmet cook. Unless you live on the edge of a fungi-producing forest, however, you're limited to what the shops and supermarkets have in stock. Use any variety or combination of mushrooms you like for this recipe.

1 boil linguini until tender.

2 sauté sliced mushrooms in a little water until tender, adding seasonings while sautéing. Be conservative with seasoning until the liquid ingredients have been added, adjusting the final spicing at the end. Add sour cream and stir. Add vegetable stock and stir. Thoroughly mix flour with warm water. Add to mushroom mixture and stir constantly until sauce thickens. Adjust seasonings and herbs. Let sit over very low heat.

3 the pasta should finish cooking about the same time as the sauce. Drain and rinse noodles and transfer to serving bowl. Ladle mushroom sauce over pasta and sprinkle with Parmesan cheese. Serve immediately.

VARIATION • *for a healthful alternative add nonfat yogurt or silky tofu in place of sour cream (see page 16).*

WINE SUGGESTIONS • *serve with Pinot Noir, medium-bodied Cabernet Sauvignon, or juicy Barbera.*

vegetable alecha (stew)

Serves 8

1 cup diced onion

2 cloves garlic, minced

4 carrots, peeled and cut

4 green bell peppers, sliced

4 potatoes, sliced

3 cups water

6 ounces tomato sauce

2 to 3 tablespoons extra-virgin
olive oil (optional)

1 to 2 teaspoons chopped fresh
ginger (or 1/2 teaspoon ground)

1 to 2 teaspoons salt

Freshly ground pepper

8 cabbage wedges, 1 inch wide

The following hearty vegetable stew is a staple of the Copts of Ethiopia. It is traditionally served on one of the many fasting days on which they are not permitted to eat meat. Ginger is what separates this stew from many American versions, giving it an exotic flavor. Ginger also acts as an antioxidant, relieves the congestion of head colds, and is reputed to help break up and expel intestinal gas.

1 in a large soup pot, sauté onions in a little water until soft but not brown. Add garlic and sauté for another minute. Add carrots, bell peppers, potatoes, water, tomato sauce, oil, ginger, salt, and pepper to taste.

2 cover and cook for 10 minutes.

3 add cabbage wedges, sprinkle with more pepper, adjust salt, and cook until vegetables are tender. Serve immediately.

NOTE • if you use fresh ginger, find a smooth looking root, as the wrinkled ones may be dried out.

WINE SUGGESTIONS • *serve with Alsatian Pinot Gris, Pinot Blanc, crisp apple-ish Chardonnay, or a Sauvignon Blanc with melony flavors.*

vegetable shepherd's pie

Serves 4 to 6

3 large red potatoes, cubed

2 1/2 cups sliced mushrooms

1 1/2 cups diced onion

3/4 cup chopped leeks

3/4 cup sliced carrots

1 cup peas

1/4 cup butter

1/4 cup brandy

Pepper

Savory salt

3 tablespoons flour

1 1/3 cups vegetable stock

2 teaspoons Worcestershire sauce

1/3 cup milk

2 teaspoons curry powder

1/2 teaspoon turmeric

2 cloves garlic, pressed or minced

Salt

In its original form, this dish was made from mutton or beef roasts left over from the traditional British Sunday dinner. The end pieces were cut up and tossed in with any leftover vegetables, topped with mashed potatoes, and baked—bland but hearty.

Amazing things can happen, however, if you rummage through the spice racks for a moment or two. In Vegetable Shepherd's Pie, curry powder, turmeric, garlic, and brandy combine to turn your leftovers into a savory gourmet experience.

1 boil cubed potatoes until tender. Set aside in water while still warm.

2 sauté mushrooms, onions, leeks, peas, and carrots in butter and a little water to keep the butter from burning until tender. Add half of brandy, and season with pepper and savory salt while cooking. As liquid collects in pan, drain off into measuring cup until you have accumulated 1/2 cup. Set liquid aside. Remove vegetables from heat when tender.

3 cook 1/2 cup buttery vegetable liquid in saucepan over medium heat until bubbly. Slowly sprinkle flour into liquid, whisking constantly to avoid clumping. When bubbly, begin slowly adding vegetable stock, whisking the entire time, and continue cooking. Add remainder of brandy, Worcestershire sauce, and season to taste with more savory salt and pepper. Cook, stirring constantly, until sauce thickens. Add sautéed vegetables to sauce and set aside.

4 drain liquid off potatoes. Beat with electric mixer with milk, curry powder, turmeric, garlic, and salt (go lightly) until smooth.

5 spoon half of the potatoes into lightly oiled 9-inch square baking dish. Pour sautéed vegetable mixture over potatoes. Spread other half of potatoes over top of vegetables and bake at 400 degrees F for 25 minutes. To allow it to set up a bit, let stand for 15 minutes before serving.

WINE SUGGESTIONS • *serve with a young Cabernet Sauvignon or round soft Merlot.*

risotto with toasted almonds and currants

Serves 4

1 medium onion, diced

1 1/2 tablespoons butter

1 1/2 tablespoons extra-virgin
   olive oil

1 cup arborio rice

3 to 4 cups vegetable stock

1/2 cup slivered almonds

1/3 cup currants

1 teaspoon turmeric

Savory salt

Cayenne (optional)

Almonds give this risotto dish both a wonderfully crunchy texture as well as a nutritional boost.

While almonds, like most nuts, are high in fat, the fat found in this nut is mostly monounsaturated. These are the fats that can help control serum cholesterol. Almonds are also high in fiber and have no cholesterol. As with most foods, consumed in moderation, almonds can be a valuable addition to the diet.

1 heat skillet over medium heat. Sauté onions in butter and olive oil and enough water to keep the mixture from drying out until tender. Add rice and stir until rice is coated with oil.

2 add vegetable stock.

3 toast slivered almonds under broiler until they begin to turn beige (1 to 2 minutes). Add almonds, currants, turmeric, and savory salt to taste, and dash of cayenne to rice. Lower heat and cook until rice is tender, stirring constantly and adding more water if necessary. Adjust salt and cayenne at the end.

VARIATION • *chopped and lightly sautéed cabbage, carrots, and broccoli complement the flavors in the rice and can be added to make a healthful entrée. Peppers, squash, peas, asparagus, and even legumes such as beans and lentils can also be added.*

WINE SUGGESTIONS • *serve with a youthful, fruity white wine, young Chardonnay, medium-weight Sauvignon Blanc, or spirited, brightly flavored Pinot Noir.*

cajun red beans and rice

Serves 8 to 10

1 pound red beans

1 large onion, diced

1 bell pepper, diced

1 package (8 ounces) meatless
  breakfast links, sliced (see note)

2 to 3 tablespoons imitation
  bacon bits

2 bay leaves

1/2 teaspoon ground oregano, or 2
  teaspoons fresh, crushed
  oregano

1/2 to 3/4 teaspoon dried ground
  thyme (or 1 tablespoon fresh
  crushed thyme)

Cayenne

Pepper

3 tablespoons extra-virgin olive oil
  (see Fats and Oils, pages xvi to xx)

Salt

4 to 6 cups cooked rice

This version of red beans and rice was concocted after attending a Cajun festival in Marin County. Zydeco music heated up an already hot day. The spicy scents of Cajun cooking wafted through the air, and I was hungry. Sniffing my way from one concession to the next, I found that virtually all Cajun food contains meat, poultry, or fish. Intoxicated with these smells, I vowed to concoct a vegetarian version of Cajun Red Beans.

To get the true flavor of this cuisine, native to the bayou country of Louisiana, you need a meat-flavored base. This is one of those times that the vegetarian cook must make a foray into the world of meat substitutes. Luckily, there is an impressive array of bacon, sausage, bologna, and salami taste-alikes made from soy available to consumers now. Many of these products were developed by Seventh-Day Adventist manufacturers who cater to the new vegetarian who still craves the taste of meat. Having been raised on beef and pork myself, there are times when I find the flavor appealing, even after many years as a vegetarian. On these occasions I'll make a dish like this one to satisfy that nostalgic craving.

1 soak beans for 2 hours. Drain off liquid and rinse.

2 sauté onion and bell pepper in a little water until tender. Add meatless sausage and continue to sauté for 1 to 2 minutes more.

3 add all other ingredients, including a generous amount of black pepper, except salt and cooked rice. Simmer 4 to 5 hours, seasoning to taste with salt at the end of cooking time. Serve in bowls over rice.

NOTE • meatless breakfast links are found in the frozen food section of the supermarket next to egg substitutes, frozen waffles, and like products.

WINE SUGGESTIONS • *serve with your favorite beer or a chilled, light red wine such as Beaujolais or Zinfandel.*

vegetable jambalaya

Serves 4 to 5

1 medium onion, sliced

1 large green bell pepper, sliced

2 stalks celery, sliced

6 ounces mushrooms, sliced

1 can (16 ounces) tomatoes

1 can (8 ounces) kidney beans

1 can (8 ounces) garbanzo beans

3 tablespoons brandy or cooking
 sherry (optional)

2 to 3 tablespoons any unrefined
 oil (optional; see Fats and Oils,
 pages xvi to xx)

1 to 2 teaspoons Worcestershire
 sauce (optional)

1 teaspoon ground dried thyme
 (or 1 tablespoon crushed fresh
 thyme)

2 cloves garlic, chopped

Generous sprinkling of paprika
 (for the top)

1 to 2 dashes cayenne

Savory salt

Freshly ground black pepper

2/3 cup water

Natives of the bayou country of Louisiana have long prided them-selves on their pungent and creative cuisine. What gives Cajun cooking its unique flavor is the marriage of European and island spices. At the base of many recipes are the classic, aromatic French herbs, such as thyme, alongside fiery cayenne and paprika. This makes for a particularly complex flavor—ideal for vegetarian cooking.

1 sauté onion and bell pepper in a little water until they begin to soften. Add celery and mushrooms and continue to sauté until all the vegetables have softened. Add tomatoes and beans and continue to cook for another few minutes.

2 add brandy, oil, Worcestershire sauce, seasonings, and water, going lightly on cayenne and savory salt. Cook over medium-low heat for another 20 minutes, stirring occasionally and adding water if mixture becomes too thick. Adjust cayenne and salt at the very end of cooking. Serve immediately over warm rice.

WINE SUGGESTIONS • *serve with a fruity Sauvignon Blanc or Beaujolais.*

pasta mediterranee

Serves 4 to 6

1 small eggplant

3 to 4 cloves garlic, finely chopped

6 cups chopped tomatoes

3 tablespoons extra-virgin olive oil

1 teaspoon herbes de Provence
   (or Italian seasoning)

3/4 cup chopped black olives

Salt

10 ounces pasta

With the proliferation of farmers' markets and produce stands across the nation comes a burgeoning variety of eggplants. One of the original species was small, white, and egg-shaped, thus the name "eggplant."

A staple of Mediterranean cuisine for centuries, this bulbous and bland vegetable adds low-calorie and lowfat bulk to a recipe. Pair it with tomatoes, olive oil, and a good herb mixture and you have the base of dozens of Mediterranean dishes.

1 cut eggplant into cubes. Sprinkle with salt and allow to stand for 30 minutes to draw out any bitterness. Rinse.

2 sauté eggplant in enough water to keep it from burning for 4 to 5 minutes. Add garlic and continue to cook for another minute. Add tomatoes, oil, and herbs. Sauté for 10 to 15 minutes until tomatoes begin to lose their moisture. Add olives and continue to cook for another 5 minutes. Season with salt.

3 cook pasta until it reaches the desired doneness, rinse, and drain. To serve, spoon sauce over pasta. (Parmesan, Asiago, or Romano cheese can be sprinkled on top if desired.)

WINE SUGGESTIONS • *serve with a light Merlot, dry rosé, or a young Chianti.*

polenta mexicana

Makes 8 servings

1/3 cup chopped green onions

1 can (4 ounces) diced green
   chiles

1/4 cup chopped black olives

1 jar (1 to 2 ounces) pimientos

1 cup polenta (5-minute type)

4 cups water

1 cup grated pepper Jack

2 teaspoons salt

Chile oil or cayenne (optional)

1 tablespoon extra-virgin olive oil
   (for "fried" version)

When it comes to polenta, there are two distinct camps—those who like it soft, like mush, and those who like it solid, usually grilled or fried. Fortunately, this recipe allows you to serve it either way.

Made from corn meal, polenta is similar to grits and can be served at any time of the day. Honey or syrup turns it into a breakfast dish while a zesty tomato sauce transforms it into a hearty entrée. Served with a bean dish, the meal contains complex carbohydrates and complete proteins. Play with it—it's worthy of a place in the vegetarian diet.

1 sauté green onions, chiles, olives, and pimientos until onions are tender. Set aside.

2 for soft version, sprinkle polenta into 4 cups boiling water, stirring constantly for about 5 minutes, until polenta reaches a mush-like texture. Remove from heat. Stir in sautéed vegetables, cheese, salt and chile oil or cayenne until cheese is melted. Serve immediately.

3 for firmer, fried style mix vegetables into soft polenta, place polenta in loaf pan after it has been cooked and refrigerate for 2 hours. Slice 1/2 thick and cook in nonstick skillet over medium-high heat in a light brushing of oil for 1 to 2 minutes. Flip and cook another couple of minutes, until polenta is thoroughly heated. Serve immediately.

VARIATION • *try it topped with green enchilada sauce.*

WINE SUGGESTIONS • *serve with a light red wine or your favorite beer.*

CANNED SUMMER SWEET BEANS •

Here's a simple canning recipe for summer-sweet, crisp green beans that has been in my friend Linda Davis' family for decades:

5 quarts broken up beans, 1 scant cup vinegar, 1/2 cup sugar, 3 tablespoons salt

Cover with water and bring to a boil. Boil for 15 minutes and put into jars while still hot. Follow canning directions. Rinse well before cooking or serving to remove the flavor of vinegar. Cook as you would fresh green beans.

----

seared marinated vegetables

Serves 4

1/4 to 1/3 cup marinade

1 to 2 squash (depending on size
   and variety), sliced

1 medium onion, sliced

1 small red bell pepper

1/4 pound mushrooms, sliced

2 cups cooked rice, 1 fresh
   baguette, or 6 ounces pasta,
   cooked

A good marinade can be one of your best kitchen helpers in turning out fast, great-tasting vegetarian cuisine. Either you can make one from scratch starting with a base of balsamic vinegar, olive oil, garlic, and any of your favorite herbs and spices, or you can go to a gourmet shop and purchase a couple of marinades to have on hand for quick meals like this one.

1 **pour** marinade over vegetables in a bowl and toss to coat. Let marinate for 5 minutes.

2 **heat** a large skillet over medium-high heat. Cook marinated vegetables until they begin to soften. Turn up the heat and continue sautéing until black spots begin to appear on the vegetables.

3 **adjust** seasonings at the end of cooking depending on the ingredients in your marinade. You can always add some freshly ground black pepper or seasoned salt to give it a little extra punch.

4 **serve** cooked vegetables over rice, or spooned onto a baguette split in half and toasted (a little cheese can be added), or toss the vegetables in with cooked pasta. These vegetables can also be served as a side dish.

WINE SUGGESTIONS • *serve with a medium-bodied Chardonnay.*

curried lentils and rice

Serves 6 to 8

1 onion, diced

1 green bell pepper, diced

2 cloves garlic, minced

1 cup brown rice (or mixed brown
    and wild rice)

1 1/2 tablespoons mustard

1 1/2 cups lentils

1 can (28 ounces) tomatoes
    (or 4 fresh tomatoes, diced)

1 1/2 teaspoons curry powder

Cayenne

Coriander

Salt and pepper

8 cups water

1/4 cup extra-virgin olive oil

There are few combinations of food that will serve you better as a dietary staple than lentils and brown rice. Higher in protein than any other member of the legume family except soybeans, lentils also contain many minerals and vitamin A. Brown rice contains many of the B vitamins, vitamin E, iron, and minerals. Both are an excellent source of fiber. Put them together and you have an almost perfectly balanced dish, which also keeps well in the refrigerator.

1 sauté onions, bell peppers, and garlic for a couple of minutes in a little water. Add rice and stir until rice is coated. Add mustard and stir.

2 add remaining ingredients, except water and oil, and stir. Add water and oil. Simmer for approximately 1 to 2 hours, checking in now and then to make sure the water level is okay. Add more water if mixture is too thick; simmer longer if it is too watery.

VARIATION • *you can add any number of fresh vegetables to the lentils during the cooking process for added flavor and texture.*

WINE SELECTION • *serve with a fruity Sauvignon Blanc, Chenin Blanc, Alsatian Pinot Blanc, or a bright, fragrant Pinot Noir served cool.*

spinach–feta crêpes

Serves 6

CRÊPES

3/4 cup flour

3/4 cup milk

2 eggs

1/4 teaspoon salt

FILLING

1 cup chopped onion

1 1/2 cups chopped mushrooms

2 cloves garlic, chopped

5 cups chopped fresh spinach

Pinch of white pepper

Pinch of nutmeg

Salt and pepper

4 ounces feta cheese, crumbled

4 ounces havarti or Monterey Jack
   cheese, grated

BÉCHAMEL SAUCE

3 tablespoons butter

4 tablespoons flour

1 1/2 cups lowfat milk

Dash of white pepper

Salt

If you're looking for a sure winner to serve for brunch, lunch, or dinner, Spinach–Feta Crêpes are it. Borrowing its full flavor from feta cheese, this is one of those vegetarian recipes that always dazzles friends and family.

Made from goat's milk, feta is white, firm, and sharp tasting. One advantage of using feta in your cooking is that, while on a par with Cheddar in fat content, only a small amount of feta is needed to achieve a full flavor. In addition, goat's milk is easier to digest for people with a lactose intolerance. This may be because the fat globules in goat's milk tend to be smaller than those in cow's milk, making it easier for the body to break them down.

1 to make the crêpes, put crêpe ingredients into blender and blend until smooth.

2 lightly brush cooking oil onto bottom of nonstick skillet over medium heat. Pour 3 to 4 tablespoons of batter in center of skillet, quickly tilting and swirling the pan until the batter has spread over the surface very thinly. Cook for 30 to 45 seconds until bottom is beige. Gently flip and cook for another 10 to 15 seconds. Turn onto a plate. Repeat until 6 crêpes are made.

3 to make crêpe filling, sauté onions, mushrooms, and garlic in a little water until onions are tender. Add spinach and cook for another minute until spinach is fairly wilted. Add white pepper, nutmeg, and salt and black pepper to taste; remove from heat.

4 mix in cheeses. Spoon approximately 1/3 cup of mixture onto each crêpe and roll. Place in baking dish with the edge of the crêpe on the bottom.

5 to make béchamel sauce, heat butter until melted but not brown or burned. Sprinkle in flour, stirring constantly. Slowly add milk, stirring constantly until thickened. Add white pepper and salt. Pour over crêpes.

6 bake at 350 degrees F for about 15 minutes, or until heated through. Do not overbake. Serve immediately.

WINE SUGGESTIONS • *serve with Sauvignon Blanc or a crisp Chardonnay.*

couscous and kidney beans

Serves 3 to 4

3/4 cup diced tomato

1/2 cup diced onion

1/2 cup diced red or green bell
   pepper

1 cup canned kidney beans,
   drained

3 tablespoons extra-virgin olive oil
   or other unrefined oil

1/2 cup corn

2 cloves garlic, minced

A few shakes of paprika

Salt and freshly ground black
   pepper

1 cup couscous (see note)

1/3 cup pistachio nuts, shelled
   (optional)

My first exposure to couscous was on a steamy hot August night in an Algerian district of Paris. Banner-size signs hung over restaurant windows to let passersby know couscous was available inside. A sample plate of what looked like loose grits with a kabob of meat laid across the top was generally in view as well. We went inside and ordered. What we got was the tiny yellow grains of pasta and legumes on the side. We waited for what we thought was the couscous—the skewered meat, as I was still eating meat back then.

To cut to the chase: We finally ate the couscous, loved it, and went home to make our own versions. Here is one of them.

1 sauté tomato, onion, and bell peppers in nonstick skillet until tender.

2 add kidney beans, oil, corn, garlic, and paprika; stir; and keep warm over low heat. Season to taste with salt and pepper.

3 prepare couscous according to package directions. Add cooked couscous to other ingredients and mix thoroughly, or top the cooked couscous with the vegetables. Sprinkle with nuts.

NOTE • couscous can be found at most supermarkets in the pasta section as well as at health food stores. A healthier version made with the bran and germ of the wheat is available in some stores as well.

WINE SUGGESTIONS • *serve with a dry rosé from the south of France or a Rhône-style rosé from California. Also, you could try a light, dry Chardonnay or an Alsatian Pinot Blanc.*

pomodoro sauce

Enough to cover 4 servings of pasta

4 to 5 fresh tomatoes, chopped

1/3 cup olive oil

2 to 3 cloves garlic, chopped

1/4 cup chopped fresh basil

   (or 1 teaspoon dried Italian

   seasoning)

Salt

Take advantage of this recipe in the summer months when inexpensive, full-flavored tomatoes are available. This timeless, classic sauce is at the base of many great recipes, including pasta dishes, pizza, and eggplant parmigiana.

If you have the time, make a large quantity and freeze it in Ziploc pouches or in airtight plastic containers for a taste of summer in the fall and winter months.

1 in a large saucepan, sauté tomatoes, oil, garlic, and basil until mixture is reduced to a dark, red color and is soft, with a small amount of liquid remaining (add a little water along the way if the liquid is evaporating too quickly). For a lighter, tarter sauce, reduce the cooking time. Season to taste with salt and cook a bit longer until the acidic taste of the tomatoes becomes richer and smoother. This sauce can be served at once over pasta or tossed into the pasta with a little freshly grated Parmesan cheese.

2 to can this sauce, fill a large pot with enough water to cover the tops of the jars you will use. Place the washed canning jars and *new* lids into the water and simmer for 15 minutes while you're making the sauce. When the sauce is done, immediately scoop into the hot, sterilized jars and put the lid and ring on top. Make sure not to tighten down the lid too hard—leave it a little bit loose. Place the jars back into the simmering water for another 15 minutes, making sure the water covers the lids. This will assure a tight seal so the sauce won't spoil.

WINE SUGGESTIONS • *serve with Orvieto, Soave, light Chardonnay, or a light, dry Italian red wine.*

FREEZING AND CANNING • *In the dead cold of winter, one of the small joys in life is to dip into summer-fresh produce that you gathered and stored yourself during the hot and bountiful days of summer. Summer-sweet corn, spiced peaches from the backyard tree, stewed summer tomatoes, and crisp green beans are just a few of the fruits and vegetables you can store away for winter. Don't be intimidated—our ancestors have been "putting up" foods from one season to another since we dried buffalo meat and herbs in caves. The main concern is to get a good seal on the jar. For this reason you'll want to follow the directions from a good book on canning to the letter. The rest is easy.*

----

olive pasta

Serves 4

6 ounces thin pasta (capellini)

1/2 cup green olives, cut into
    quarters (see note)

1/2 cup black olives, cut into
    quarters

1/3 cup red bell pepper, diced

1/3 cup green bell pepper, diced

2 cloves garlic, pressed or minced

Dash of cayenne

Paprika

1/4 to 1/2 teaspoon salt

1 1/2 tablespoons flour

1/4 to 1/3 cup extra-virgin olive oil

1/3 to 1/2 cup freshly grated
    Parmesan cheese

Once upon a time I suppose this would have been the pasta of kings. As one of the oldest documented foods on the planet, olives have been a symbol of health, wealth, peace, and goodwill for millennia. Homer referred to them in *The Iliad*. Pickled olives were found in excavations at Pompeii. So popular was olive oil, in fact, that the Romans believed the path to a long and pleasant life was dependent on two fluids: "Wine within, and (olive) oil without."

The use of olives in this recipe was the inspiration of my dear friend Clint. Adding a little flour to the olive oil at the end of sautéing makes for a light, quick, no-fuss coating without the heaviness of a sauce. This is a favorite of mine.

1 cook the pasta to desired doneness. Drain, rinse in cold water, and set aside.

2 sauté olives, peppers, and garlic in a little water over medium heat until peppers are soft.

3 in a small bowl, mix cayenne, paprika (use 2 to 3 dashes), and salt with the flour. Add oil to vegetables. Sprinkle flour mixture over the olive and peppers and stir. Continue cooking over low heat for a few seconds.

4 add the pasta and toss until all noodles are coated and olives are spread throughout. Toss the Parmesan cheese into pasta at the last minute and serve immediately.

NOTE • use olives packaged in jars rather than cans if possible. Canned olives tend to have a "tinny" taste.

WINE SUGGESTIONS • *serve with chilled young chianti, Orvieto, or Soave.*

ratatouille scramble

Serves 4 to 5

1 large potato, cut into small cubes

3 to 4 tablespoons olive oil

1/2 cup vegetable broth

1 small onion

1/2 medium bell pepper

1 medium tomato, chopped

6 ounces mushrooms, sliced

2 small squash (zucchini, crookneck, or other variety)

Italian seasonings (or herbes de
Provence)

Salt and pepper

6 eggs, beaten

4 ounces grated Parmesan,
Romano, or Asiago

Open your refrigerator, look around for any produce that hasn't "turned," chop it up, and throw it in a skillet and you have the makings of what the French call ratatouille. Loosely speaking, ratatouille means "stew of leftovers," despite what some pricey French restaurants would have you believe. While ratatouille is generally made from tomatoes, onions, peppers, eggplant, and squash, you can use whatever produce you like.

To make this dish a little heartier, the recipe calls for eggs and cheese, rather than leftover pieces of meat as did the original 1877 recipe from Nice, France. You can also serve it without eggs or cheese.

1 sauté potatoes in olive oil and vegetable broth for 2 to 3 minutes. Add onion and bell pepper and continue to sauté, adding water as mixture dries to keep oil from overheating. Add tomatoes and mushrooms and sauté a few more minutes. Add squash and seasonings to taste and continue to sauté until squash is tender but not mushy.

2 stir in eggs and cheese and cook until eggs are firm, turning constantly. Serve immediately. Bon appétit!

NOTE • herbes de Provence are similar to Italian seasoning but also include certain herbs grown in the Provence region of southern France. These herbs give the blend a scent reminiscent of anise (licorice). Herbes de Provence can be found at any gourmet store, usually packaged in a small clay pot.

WINE SUGGESTIONS • *serve with a Provence red or light Merlot.*

gumbo stew

Serves 6 to 8

2 cups diced onion

6 cups vegetable stock

2 cloves garlic, chopped

2/3 cup diced celery

1/2 cup diced bell pepper

2 1/2 cups diced tomatoes

2 tablespoons extra-virgin olive oil
   (optional)

2 cups chopped okra (frozen or
   fresh)

2/3 cup rice

5 meatless breakfast links

1 1/2 teaspoons chili powder

1 teaspoon dried parsley

1/2 to 3/4 teaspoon thyme

Generous sprinkling of paprika

Salt (or seasoned salt)

Dash of cayenne

Black pepper

Spicing options: filé powder,
   Tabasco, Worcestershire sauce,
   and basil

My love affair with gumbo began with the little red and white cans in the grocery store—Campbell's chicken gumbo soup. For many of us, the canned version remains our only exposure to this New Orleans treasure. What distinguishes gumbo from an ordinary vegetable soup or stew is the addition of okra, rice, thyme, and peppery spices. Beyond that, just about anything goes into spicing this dish.

This recipe is part of my concession to faux meats. While not essential, it is hard to imagine much of the famous bayou cooking without a hint of sausage. I use imitation breakfast links, which are generally found in the freezer section of the supermarket with other breakfast foods. They are amazingly authentic tasting with none of the cholesterol, gristle, and grease found in the real thing.

1 in a large soup pot, sauté onions in a little of the vegetable stock until they begin to turn transparent. Add garlic, celery, bell pepper, and tomatoes and continue to sauté until celery is tender.

2 add vegetable stock, oil, okra, and rice. Continue cooking.

3 microwave or sauté the meatless breakfast links according to package directions. Break up into small pieces and add to soup.

4 begin adding spices, going lightly on the salt, cayenne, and black pepper until the end. When rice is tender, adjust the seasonings to your taste. Serve immediately.

WINE SUGGESTIONS • *serve with a chilled light red or Beaujolais.*

pasta primavera with red sauce

Serves 4 to 6

3 1/2 pounds tomatoes, finely
  chopped

3 cloves garlic, minced

3 to 4 tablespoons olive oil

2 to 3 teaspoons dried basil

1/2 teaspoon dried thyme

1/4 teaspoon ground cinnamon

Salt and pepper

1 teaspoon vanilla

1 1/2 cups sliced mushrooms

1 1/2 cups cut-up broccoli

1 cup snow peas, strings removed

Savory salt

10 to 12 ounces pasta

Parmesan cheese, grated
  (optional)

While those succulent red globes of summer are certainly the first choice for this tomato-based sauce, Roma tomatoes will make a good substitute the remainder of the year.

The tougher quality of the Roma allows the grower to leave it on the vine longer, thus gaining more flavor than its spherical counterparts in the cloudy, cold months.

1 sauté the tomatoes and garlic in olive oil and a little water over medium heat along with seasonings, waiting until the end to make final adjustments with salt and pepper. Cook tomatoes over medium heat for about 30 minutes, stirring occasionally, adding water along the way, until they are greatly reduced and have lost the acidic taste. Reducing the liquid makes for a richer tomato flavor, but this is a matter of taste. You can lightly cook the tomatoes for a fresher, lighter sauce as well. During the last few minutes of cooking, add vanilla.

2 in a separate pot, steam mushrooms, broccoli, and snow peas until they reach desired doneness. Sprinkle vegetables lightly with savory salt. Add vegetables to the tomato sauce and keep warm.

3 meanwhile, boil noodles until tender. Drain and rinse. Top with sauce and sprinkle with Parmesan.

WINE SUGGESTIONS • *serve with a young Chianti or full-bodied Italian white.*

caramelized onion and cheddar crêpes

Serves 3 to 6

1 recipe of crêpes from
　Spinach–Feta Crêpes
　(pages 162 to 163)

FILLING

1 large onion, thinly sliced

2 tablespoons butter

1/2 pound mushrooms, thinly
　sliced

1 teaspoon dried crushed thyme

BÉCHAMEL SAUCE

3 tablespoons butter

1/4 cup flour

1 1/2 cups lowfat milk

1 1/2 tablespoons spicy prepared
　mustard

1/2 to 1 teaspoon freshly ground
　black pepper

1 teaspoon ground cumin

1 1/2 cups grated sharp Cheddar
　cheese

2 apples, cored and sliced

This is a special occasion dish—rich in flavor, but high in fat. This would not be recommended for those on a fat-restricted diet or for those with high cholesterol.

1 prepare crêpes according to instructions for Spinach–Feta Crêpes (pages 162–163).

2 sauté onions in butter and a little water until onions begin to soften. Add mushrooms and thyme and continue to sauté until mushrooms are tender.

3 to make béchamel sauce, melt 3 tablespoons butter in small pot. Do not burn butter. Sprinkle flour over butter and stir until blended and bubbly. Slowly add milk, stirring constantly with a whisk to keep lumps from forming. Add mustard, black pepper, and cumin and stir.

4 place equal portions of cheese on each of 6 crêpes. Place equal portions of mushroom mixture on top of cheese. Spoon equal amounts of béchamel sauce onto mushrooms, reserving half of the sauce. Roll the crêpes and place in baking dish. Drizzle remaining sauce on top of crêpes and bake at 350 degrees F for 20 minutes. If sauce becomes too thick, add a little milk to thin it out so it drizzles easily over crêpes. Serve with sliced apples.

WINE SUGGESTION • *serve with a chilled, youthful light red wine.*

herbed vegetable pot pie

Serves 4 to 6

1 1/4 cups diced potatoes

2 cups sliced mushrooms

1 cup chopped leeks

1 cup corn (fresh or frozen)

3/4 cup sliced baby carrots

4 tablespoons butter

1/2 cup vegetable broth

1/2 to 1 teaspoon Italian seasoning
   (or fines herbes to taste)

Freshly ground black pepper

Pinch of white pepper

Savory salt (or salt)

5 tablespoons flour

2 tablespoons water

2 cups lowfat milk or soy milk

Salt

1 teaspoon Worcestershire sauce

1 pie crust, fresh or premade (or 6
   puff pastry shells; see variation)

Raised by a modern woman of the '50s, our family put Swanson's pot pies right at the top of the fine foods list. Mom was particularly happy about the ease of this new "heat and serve" option. With nothing to compare it to, we were more than content with the flavor of this creamy, crusty comfort food.

1 sauté vegetables in 1 tablespoon butter and vegetable broth, starting with potatoes, until vegetables are crisp-tender. Add seasonings, being generous with the Italian seasoning and black and white peppers.

2 melt the remaining 3 tablespoons of butter in a saucepan over medium heat. Do not burn butter. Sprinkle half of the flour into melted butter, stirring quickly. Add 2 tablespoons water to remaining flour and mix to make a thin paste; set aside. Add the milk slowly, stirring constantly, until the sauce thickens. (Add more milk if it is too thick, as it will thicken during baking.)

3 pour sauce over vegetables and add more salt if necessary. Add Worcestershire.

4 pour vegetable filling into a 9-inch square baking dish. Place pie crust over top, sealing to the edges of dish. Bake at 400 degrees F for 20 to 25 minutes.

VARIATION • *bake puff pastry shells according to package directions. Spoon heated vegetable filling into shells and serve.*

WINE SUGGESTIONS • *serve with an oaky Chardonnay, light Pinot Noir, or medium Merlot.*

PRESERVING SUMMER SWEET CORN • One of my favorite gardening authorities, Joe Patitucci, grows just about everything on six acres of prime growing land in the fertile Sacramento Valley right in the middle of a densely populated suburb. He cans and freezes his produce to last until the following summer and this is his foolproof method for preserving the sweet corn of summer for use in the cold winter months. (If you are a fresh-ingredients-only cook, you might chafe a bit at this—he uses 7-Up*). Directions: In a freezer bag filled with corn kernels stripped from the cob, cover the corn with 7-Up or a "natural" brand of lemon-lime soft drink. Seal and freeze. When you are ready to use the corn, thaw, rinse and use. It really does keep a good amount of its crispness.

----

* I haven't tried this, but, what if you substituted the soft drink with sparkling mineral water sweetened with sugar or honey and followed the same directions? You would eliminate the chemicals found in even "natural" soft drinks.

eggplant stir-fry

Serves 4

2 tablespoons unrefined peanut oil

1 medium eggplant, cubed

1/4 cup sliced onion

2/3 cup snow peas, ends and
   strings removed

2 cups sliced mushrooms

3 cloves garlic, minced

2 to 3 tablespoons shoyu

2 splashes Worcestershire sauce

Juice of 1/2 lemon

Dash of cayenne

1 1/2 cups bean sprouts

3 cups cooked rice

Sunflower seeds

If you enjoy the flavors of Asian cooking, it is worth your while to invest in a bottle of shoyu. Unlike other supermarket soy sauces, shoyu is a naturally fermented soy sauce that uses the whole soybean. The traditional two-year shoyu-making process makes for a much richer and mellower soy sauce.

1 heat peanut oil and some water in wok or skillet over medium-high heat. Cook eggplant until it softens.

2 add the rest of the vegetables (except bean sprouts) and garlic and cook, stirring and tossing constantly for 1 to 2 minutes. Add water if mixture dries out, overheating the oil. Add shoyu, Worcestershire sauce, lemon juice, and cayenne. Add sprouts and continue to toss. Cook for another few seconds until sprouts begin to wilt.

3 serve hot over rice. Sprinkle with sunflower seeds for additional texture and protein.

WINE SUGGESTIONS • *serve with a full-bodied Sauvignon Blanc or Asian beer.*

ranchero risotto

Serves 4

1 cup chopped onion

1 to 2 cloves garlic, minced

1 medium red bell pepper

1 cup fresh corn kernels (or
  frozen)

1/3 cup chopped fresh basil
  (or 2 teaspoons dried)

1 1/2 tablespoons olive oil

Dash of cayenne

1 cup arborio rice

2 cups vegetable stock

1/2 cup dry white wine

1/2 to 1 cup water

1/2 teaspoon salt

1/2 cup coarsely grated Parmesan
  cheese

Here's yet another California variation of the classic Italian dish, risotto. Capitalizing on the flavors and textures of red bell pepper and corn, this version of risotto brings the flavor of the Southwest together with the classic dry white wine and Parmesan of Italy to make a wonderful entrée or side dish.

1 sauté onion, garlic, bell pepper, corn, and basil in olive oil and a little water until vegetables begin to soften.

2 add cayenne and rice and stir.

3 add vegetable stock and wine and cook over medium or medium-low heat while the liquid absorbs. Taste along the way for desired texture. If you would like it on the soft side, add water and continue to cook and stir until rice reaches the correct texture. Add salt at the end of cooking, along with Parmesan cheese. Serve hot.

WINE SUGGESTIONS • *serve with Valpolicella or another light Italian red wine or try a full-bodied Chardonnay.*

stuffed zucchini

Serves 2 to 3

3 average zucchini (or 1 very large
zucchini)

2/3 cup diced onion

2/3 cup chopped mushrooms

1 to 2 tablespoons extra-virgin
olive oil

Italian seasonings (basil, oregano,
thyme)

Salt and pepper

2/3 cup cooked rice

2 to 3 tablespoons grated
Parmesan cheese (optional)

1 1/2 cups V-8 juice

Three hints: It's big, green, and generally unsolicited. Yes, it's an offering of zucchini from the backyard of a well-intentioned neighbor or friend. The giver often accompanies the offering with a comment like, "Can you believe the *size* of this?"

If you're not sure what to do with your unsolicited zucchini, this recipe will help.

1 boil the zucchini, whole, until tender, about 7 to 10 minutes. Set aside.

2 sauté onion and mushrooms in olive oil and a little water until tender. Add Italian seasonings, salt, and pepper (be generous with seasonings as the main ingredients are bland). Stir in rice.

3 slice zucchini in half lengthwise. Scoop out tender, seeded part, leaving a shell. Chop up the pulp and add to rice mixture. Stir in Parmesan cheese.

4 spoon mixture into zucchini shells. Pour V-8 juice over the top, allowing it to spill over into the baking dish. Bake at 375 degrees F for 20 to 25 minutes. Serve hot, spooning extra juice over the top.

WINE SUGGESTION • *serve with a full-bodied white wine.*

pasta crema aurora

Serves 6 to 8

10 to 12 ounces penne pasta

2/3 cup chopped onion

2 cloves garlic, finely chopped or
   pressed

6 cups diced tomatoes

2 to 3 tablespoons dry white
   vermouth

1 teaspoon herbes de Provence

Salt

1 cup grated sharp Cheddar
   cheese, fontina, or aged Gouda

1/2 cup half-and-half

One of the more elegant pasta dishes, this recipe relies on the combination of tomatoes and cream. Rich and aromatic, this is perfect for serving at a dinner party as a side dish or an entrée.

1 cook penne until it reaches desired doneness. Drain.

2 meanwhile, sauté onion and garlic in a little water until tender. Add tomatoes, vermouth, and herbes de Provence and continue to sauté until tomatoes are soft and liquid is reduced to small amount. Salt to taste.

3 reduce heat to low and add cheese a little at a time, stirring constantly. When all of the cheese has been added, slowly add the half-and-half, stirring constantly (see note). Simmer for a couple of minutes until mixture is well blended and bubbly. Remove from heat. Pour over pasta and toss until pasta is well coated. Serve hot.

NOTE • add a little baking soda to half-and-half to avoid having the half-and-half "break up" when introduced into the tomato base (see page 118).

WINE SUGGESTIONS • *serve with Orvieto, Soave, a light Sauvignon Blanc, or a light, dry rosé from the south of France.*

enchiladas verde

Serves 5 to 10

1 cup diced onions

1/2 cup diced bell peppers

2 tablespoons any unrefined oil

1 cup corn

1 cup seasoned pinto or chili
  beans

1/3 cup diced green chiles

1 can (2 1/4 ounces) chopped
  olives

1/4 cup taco sauce

1/3 cup water

2 tablespoons masa (finely ground
  cornmeal)

Chili powder

Salt

10 large corn tortillas

8 ounces grated Monterey Jack
  cheese or pepper Jack
  (optional)

1 large can green enchilada sauce

Mexican cuisine is often a favorite among vegetarians because, with a little imagination, a burrito, tostada, or enchilada can be a highly flavorful and nutritious meal in itself.

One of the tricks to making enchiladas is keeping the tortillas soft and malleable while you are working with and baking them. This is traditionally done by dropping the tortilla into oil, over medium heat, and removing it very quickly. To minimize the amount of oil in the recipe, this one calls for steaming the tortillas one at a time.

1 sauté onions and diced bell peppers in oil and a little water until tender. Add corn, beans, chiles, olives, taco sauce, and water. Heat until bubbly and sprinkle in masa. Cook until mixture thickens (this will happen quickly). Add chili powder and salt to taste. Set aside.

2 heat water in a pot or pan with a steaming basket. One at a time, steam each tortilla until soft but not gooey, and immediately fill.

3 spoon filling onto 1 tortilla at a time and top with a small amount of cheese. Roll and place in baking dish, with the exposed edge facing down. Repeat until all 10 tortillas are used. Spoon green enchilada sauce over top. Bake at 400 degrees F for about 15 minutes. Serve hot.

WINE SUGGESTIONS • *serve with your favorite beer or flavorful Sauvignon Blanc.*

zucchini and mushroom melt

Serves 4

1/2 pound mushrooms, sliced

2 cloves garlic, minced or pressed

1 tablespoon butter (or olive oil)

4 medium zucchini (or other favorite summer variety), sliced

1/2 teaspoon Italian seasoning (or herbes de Provence)

Juice of 1/2 lemon

Salt or seasoning salt

1/2 cup Parmesan or Asiago cheese (optional)

If you're wondering what to do with all those beautiful squash you bought at the farmers' market, this recipe can use just about any variety of summer squash.

1 sauté mushrooms and garlic in butter or oil with a little water in a nonstick skillet over medium heat until mushrooms begin to soften. Add zucchini and herbs and continue to sauté until zucchini is just barely soft. Do not overcook squash. Sprinkle with lemon juice and salt to taste.

2 sprinkle with cheese and cover. Continue to cook over reduced heat for another minute or so until cheese is melted. Serve hot.

WINE SUGGESTIONS • *serve with a French Chardonnay or crisp Chardonnay.*

side dishes and accompaniments

couscous

scorched teriyaki green beans

greens with toasted sesame seeds

basic pinto beans

"the day after" beans

tangy potato–broccoli bake

aloo gobi

sautéed red chard and onions

cajun cauliflower and potatoes

corn cakes with chiles and squash

dahl

bavarian sauerkraut

jalapeño potatoes

corn bread 'n apple stuffing

brown onion gravy

paprika asparagus

baked beans with pineapple

sweet potato casserole

curried sweet potato pancakes

paratha

focaccia with rosemary and green olives

lori's acorn squash

carrot–orange soufflé

jackie's zucchini–salsa sauté

scalloped potatoes with leeks and chives

baby crookneck squash

east indian creamed spinach

spicy rice

couscous

Serves 4 to 6

1/2 cup diced green bell pepper

1/2 cup diced onion

1 stalk celery, sliced or chopped

1 clove garlic, minced

1/4 teaspoon seasoned salt

1/4 teaspoon turmeric

1 cup couscous

1 cup vegetable stock, heated
  to boiling

1 tablespoon extra-virgin olive oil

Many people have thought couscous to be a whole grain. In fact, this granular carbohydrate substance is made from wheat flour and is simply a tiny piece of pasta. Traditionally only the refined endosperm (inside starch) of durum wheat has been used, but more companies are offering whole-grain couscous now. The whole-grain version is high in protein and a nutritious base for a meal.

Many Middle Eastern dishes rely on a basic couscous as a bed for other foods such as meat or vegetables. Onion, pepper, and celery give this basic couscous recipe enough substance, however, that it can stand alone as a side dish or be used under vegetables, ragout, or ratatouille.

1 sauté vegetables and garlic in a little water until tender. Remove from heat.

2 add seasoned salt and turmeric.

3 add couscous and stir until ingredients are well mixed.

4 pour in boiling hot stock and oil.

5 cover and allow to stand for 5 minutes until couscous has absorbed all the liquid. Serve hot.

scorched teriyaki green beans

Serves 4

1 pound green beans, ends and
strings removed
3 tablespoons Gourmet Teriyaki
Sauce (page 52)

With the West Coast openings of many restaurants specializing in foods from the Pacific Rim, there is no shortage of culinary inspiration. This recipe was inspired by a similar dish served at a California–Vietnamese restaurant in San Francisco. Its success is dependent upon the care you put into making the teriyaki sauce, but it's worth it, and the sauce can be used for many other dishes. Keep in mind that teriyaki sauce can burn easily because of the honey or sugars used in its production. Add it at the very end of the cooking process to avoid burning.

1 in a skillet, sauté beans in water, adding water along the way, until beans are the desired texture. Allow water to evaporate, then continue to cook until black spots appear on most of the beans. Toss regularly during the cooking process until beans begin to soften.

2 reduce heat, add teriyaki sauce and an equal amount of water, and continue to toss and cook for another 30 to 60 seconds, taking care not to let the sauce burn. Serve hot.

greens with toasted sesame seeds

Serves 4

1 bunch greens (chard, spinach,
   collard, or mustard)

1 ounce sesame seeds

1 to 2 cloves garlic, minced

2 tablespoons unrefined peanut oil

1/4 cup vegetable stock

2 tablespoons tahini

2 generous splashes shoyu

Unfortunately, lingering memories of canned and frozen spinach discourage many of us from diving into a fresh bunch of greens. I too was less than thrilled to cook with greens for many years. It wasn't until I joined a cooperative farm, which delivers whatever is in season, that I discovered the wonder of fresh greens.

This particular recipe for greens was inspired by a dish served to us by a friend of ours who is a sushi chef in San Francisco. It is a very simple dish, but unique, with its wonderfully rich sesame flavor.

1 wash greens thoroughly.

2 toast sesame seeds in a skillet over medium heat, watching and stirring until they become golden in color.

3 sauté garlic in oil and vegetable stock over medium heat for 30 to 60 seconds. Add tahini and stir for a few seconds.

4 add greens and sesame seeds and cook for a minute or so, tossing constantly until greens are wilted. Splash with shoyu. Remove from heat and serve.

basic pinto beans

Serves 8

2 quarts water

1 pound pinto beans, rinsed

2 tablespoons extra-virgin olive oil

1 teaspoon chili powder

1/2 teaspoon hickory salt

Cayenne

Salt

Just as the name implies, this tasty but simple bean recipe can be served alone with a good piece of corn bread and a salad or used in burritos, soups, and more.

1 bring water to a boil and add beans and remaining ingredients except salt. Cook over low heat for 2 to 3 hours, checking along the way to ensure that there is adequate liquid. The finished product should be the texture of a soup. Add salt at the end of cooking. The "soup" will thicken as it cools. Serve hot.

2 leftover beans can be used to top baked potatoes, over rice, as a burrito filling, as refried beans, or in other soups.

NO NEED TO SOAK BEANS • *According to the food editors at* Saveur, *a gourmet cooking magazine, it is not necessary to soak beans before use. It is thought that if the beans are soaked they will cook faster and the gas-producing agents in the beans will be reduced. In fact, the beans will only cook about 15 minutes faster by soaking them and the reduction in the oligosaccharides (the gas-producing sugars) is only slightly reduced, while some of the beans nutrients are stripped away in the process. (And all this time I thought I was cheating by not soaking the beans first!) It is, however, a good idea to rinse the beans before use.*

NOTE: some say the seaweed kombu will reduce the "gas" in beans if you cook it with the beans.

"the day after" beans

Serves 4

1 cup diced onion

1 tablespoon any unrefined oil

6 to 8 strips meatless bacon,
   cut up

2 cups Basic Pinto Beans
   (page 190)

2/3 cup tomato sauce

After you have had enough Basic Pinto Beans, you can transform them into a wonderful baked bean–style dish.

1 sauté onions in oil and a little water until soft. Add meatless bacon and continue to cook until it is slightly crispy.

2 add beans and tomato sauce and continue to cook at a low simmer. Add water if mixture becomes too thick. Serve hot.

tangy potato–broccoli bake

Serves 6

1 1/2 pounds potatoes

1 small bunch broccoli, cut up

3/4 cup milk or soy milk

1 clove garlic, minced

1 1/2 to 2 tablespoons spicy
    mustard

Pinch of cayenne

3/4 teaspoon salt

1 3/4 cups grated sharp Cheddar
    cheese

2 tablespoons butter

Light as a cloud, this cheesy and tangy potato dish makes an excellent side dish, or it can be used as a light entrée along with a salad if served in larger portions.

1 heat oven to 400 degrees F.

2 peel and cut up potatoes. Boil in lightly salted water until tender. Drain off water.

3 steam or boil broccoli until tender. Place cooked broccoli along with half of the milk into a blender and purée until smooth.

4 add to potatoes. Add remainder of the milk and beat with an electric mixer, adding garlic, mustard, cayenne, and salt along the way. Add 1 1/4 cups of the grated cheese and continue mixing for another 30 seconds. If mixture is too heavy or sticky, add more milk slowly until mixture becomes light and fluffy.

5 put butter in 8- or 9-inch square baking dish and heat in oven until butter is melted. Remove from oven and add potato mixture. Top with remaining cheese and bake for 15 to 20 minutes. Serve hot.

NOTE • this recipe can also be baked and served in individual baking dishes for a nice presentation.

aloo gobi

Serves 6 to 8

1/2 onion, chopped

4 cloves garlic, chopped

1 tablespoon fresh ginger, chopped

1 1/2 teaspoons salt

1 teaspoon turmeric

1/2 teaspoon paprika

1 tomato, chopped

3 tablespoons extra-virgin olive oil

3 small potatoes, cubed

1 head cauliflower, cut up

1/2 cup tomato sauce

Cayenne

Aloo Gobi is a staple of the East Indian diet and has much to offer Westerners. Flavored with garlic, ginger, onion, and spicy, ground peppers, this cauliflower and potato dish is not only filling but exceptionally healthful. It is well matched with the Raitziki appetizer (page 13), Dahl (page 198), and Paratha (pages 208 to 209) for a very filling Indian meal.

1 sauté onions, garlic, and ginger in a little water until onions are tender. Add salt, turmeric, and paprika and stir.

2 add tomato and oil and continue to cook, stirring, for 1 to 2 minutes. Add potatoes and sauté for about 5 minutes, adding a little water to keep mixture from drying out and sticking.

3 add cauliflower and tomato sauce and cook for another 10 to 15 minutes. Season to taste with cayenne. Serve hot.

sautéed red chard and onions

Serves 4

1 bunch red chard, washed and
   stems removed
1/2 cup chopped onions
1 to 2 tablespoons olive oil
Juice of 1/2 lemon
Salt
1/2 teaspoon honey

If your exposure to greens growing up was limited to canned spinach, you were undoubtedly surprised to find the pleasant, full, fresh flavor of real greens once you tried them. This recipe is simple and allows the full flavor of the greens to come through, only slightly enhanced by the onion, lemon, and honey.

As with spinach, chard is high in vitamins and minerals and is best served alongside another dish such as peppers or cauliflower. These foods have high levels of vitamin C, which allows for maximum absorption of the iron and minerals in the greens.

1 chop chard into small pieces.

2 sauté onions in olive oil and a little water until tender. Add chard and toss quickly while cooking over medium heat.

3 quickly squeeze lemon juice over chard and season with salt to taste. Remove from heat before chard becomes limp.

4 stir in honey to cut any remaining bitterness. Serve hot.

cajun cauliflower and potatoes

Serves 4

1 cup minced onions

1 large potato, cubed

1 to 2 cloves garlic, minced or
   pressed

2 tablespoons unrefined oil

1/2 cup vegetable stock

1 tablespoon freshly squeezed
   lemon juice

1 1/2 teaspoons Cajun seasoning
   (or cayenne, paprika, and
   thyme)

Salt

Freshly ground black pepper

3 cups cauliflower, broken into
   small pieces

Let's sing the virtues of cauliflower for a moment: It is high in cancer-fighting nutrients, helps lower blood pressure, builds red blood cells, boosts the immune system, and is great for weight loss.

Everything else in this recipe is just for flavor, fun, and bulk.

1 sauté onions, potato, and garlic in oil and a little vegetable stock until onions are tender.

2 add remaining vegetable stock, lemon juice, Cajun spices, and salt and pepper to taste; stir. Add cauliflower. Cook over medium-low heat for about 30 minutes, or until potatoes and cauliflower are tender, adding water along the way if the mixture becomes too dry. Serve hot.

corn cakes with chiles and squash

Makes 6 to 8 corn cakes

1 cup cubed sunblossom squash
(1/2-inch cubes)

1 tablespoon finely chopped fresh
jalapeño or poblano chile

Seasoned salt

2/3 cup cornmeal

2/3 cup flour

2 teaspoons baking powder

1/2 teaspoon salt

1 small egg

2/3 cup milk or soy milk

1/4 cup unrefined vegetable oil

2 tablespoons honey

1/2 cup grated smoked Gouda
cheese (or smoked Cheddar)

This is one of my all-time favorite recipes.

The original version of these corn cakes used a mild cheese and
was not all that impressive. I finally hit on smoked Gouda and it
worked. The only drawback is that smoked Gouda is Holland's version of American cheese—it is a processed cheese. Its flavor, however, is hard to match. A good second here would be smoked
Cheddar.

1 sauté squash and chiles in a little water over medium-high
heat for about 2 minutes. Add seasoned salt to taste. Set aside.

2 in a mixing bowl, combine cornmeal, flour, baking powder,
and salt. In a separate cup or small bowl, lightly beat egg and milk
together. Add milk–egg mixture, 1/4 cup vegetable oil, and
honey to dry ingredients and stir until batter is smooth, about 30
to 40 strokes.

3 add squash mixture and cheese to batter.

4 brush the bottom of a nonstick skillet with a small amount of oil over medium heat and spoon portions of batter equaling 2 tablespoons per pancake into heated skillet. Cook each corn cake until both sides have browned. Serve immediately.

N O T E • if sunblossom squash is not available, use any summer variety, making sure not to overcook the softer varieties.

dahl

Serves 6 to 8

6 cups water

1 1/2 cups lentils

1 teaspoon salt

1/2 teaspoon turmeric

1/2 onion, chopped

5 cloves garlic, chopped

1 tablespoon fresh ginger, chopped

1/2 teaspoon garam masala (see
  note)

1/2 teaspoon ground coriander

1/2 teaspoon ground cumin

Cayenne

1/2 tomato, chopped

2 tablespoons tomato sauce

Parsley or cilantro (for garnish),
  optional

This is the traditional lentil dish of India. Dahl is made from any variety of lentils and can be made thin as a soup, or thick, mopped up with Chapati (pages 208 to 209) or a tortilla. The cooking time will depend on the type of lentil you choose. The whole, brown lentil takes the longest, while the split, hulled red or yellow lentil takes only 30 minutes to cook.

1 heat water and boil lentils with salt and turmeric until they reach a creamy, soupy consistency.

2 sauté onions, garlic, and ginger in a little water until soft and browned. Add garam masala, coriander, cumin, and cayenne to taste and cook for 1 minute. Add tomato and cook until tomato is soft. Add tomato sauce and cook for another minute.

3 add to cooked lentils and stir. Garnish with parsley or cilantro.

NOTE • garam masala is a spice combination that can be found in Indian grocery, gourmet, or import stores.

bavarian sauerkraut

Makes 2 cups

1 can or bottle (16 ounces) sauer-
    kraut, drained and rinsed
1/2 cup white wine
1/2 cup chopped onion
1/4 cup chopped apple
10 juniper berries
Salt and pepper
1 tablespoon oil with a dash of
    hickory salt (optional)

We have Norbert Pappenberger, my brother-in-law, to thank for this wonderful sauerkraut from his native Germany.

1 put sauerkraut in a pot and add water until the sauerkraut is covered.

2 add remaining ingredients and simmer for 1 1/2 to 2 hours, adding water as needed to keep mixture from scorching. Discard juniper berries. Serve hot or cold.

jalapeño potatoes

Serves 4

1 cup diced onion

1 jalapeño, finely chopped

2 tablespoons olive oil

5 cups very thinly sliced potatoes

Savory salt (or garlic salt)

Flour

1/4 cup sour cream

1/4 cup milk, heated

1/2 cup grated extra-sharp
   Cheddar cheese

When choosing your jalapeño peppers, consider the season. If it is the height of summer, they are *hot*. You'll want to adjust the amount of jalapeños in this recipe accordingly.

1 sauté onion and jalapeño in a little water over medium heat until the onions are tender. Add oil and remove from heat.

2 oil a 9-inch square baking pan. Place a layer of potatoes on the bottom of the pan. Sprinkle with savory salt and a light dusting of flour.

3 spoon half of the onion and jalapeño mixture over potatoes. Dot with half of the sour cream. Repeat process with another layer, reserving just enough potatoes to make a thin top layer. Layer the remaining potatoes on top, sprinkle with savory salt, slowly pour heated milk over the top, and cover with Cheddar cheese.

4 bake at 325 degrees F for 1 hour and 20 minutes. Serve hot.

corn bread 'n apple stuffing

Serves 10 to 12

1 large onion, diced

3 stalks celery, diced

2 to 3 cups water

2 cups apples, chopped

4 cups dried bread cubes

4 cups corn bread, broken up

1/3 cup butter, melted

1 package (8 ounces) meatless
  breakfast links

2 tablespoons ground rubbed sage

Salt and pepper

Brown Onion Gravy (page 202),
  optional

Thanksgiving can be a real problem for vegetarians. Everybody is helping themselves to steamy mounds of stuffing and gravy as the vegetarian watches wistfully. Take heart; it doesn't have to be that way!

This stuffing recipe uses vegetable-based "sausage" to give it a hearty and spicy holiday flavor. To give it the moisture usually derived from baking it inside the turkey, you bake it in a hollowed-out pumpkin, which also makes a festive serving dish.

1 boil onion and celery in water until tender. Strain vegetables, reserving liquid.

2 toss all ingredients together, except spices and gravy. Sprinkle in spices, tasting as you go, making sure to add plenty of pepper.

3 moisten mixture with 1/2 to 1 cup of the liquid the vegetables were boiled in. Stuff into pulp-free pumpkin. Bake for 2 to 3 hours at 350 degrees F. For presentation, place stuffing inside the pumpkin on a serving dish surrounded with fresh parsley. Sprinkle fresh cranberries around the base. Serve with Brown Onion Gravy.

NOTE • you will find a few different brands of vegetarian gravy mixes at most health food stores. Doctor them up as you like.

brown onion gravy

Makes 1 1/2 to 2 cups

3 tablespoons butter

1 medium onion, thinly sliced

3 tablespoons flour

1 1/2 to 2 cups water

1 vegetarian bouillon cube or 1
    tablespoon powdered broth

Salt

Freshly ground pepper

This vegetarian gravy will give you all the satisfaction of the kind that follows the mashed potatoes around the table during holiday dinners.

1 heat butter and sauté onion over medium heat until transparent.

2 sprinkle flour over onion and stir until evenly coated and bubbly.

3 slowly add water and bouillon cube, stirring constantly, until desired consistency is reached.

4 salt and pepper to taste.

paprika asparagus

Serves 3 to 4

1/2 pound asparagus tips
2 tablespoons butter
2 pinches paprika
Grated Parmesan
Salt (optional)

Joe Patitucci's family is from Calabria, a city where people know what to do with produce. Joe and his family eventually came to America and began growing produce in the Bread Basket area of California. Today, if you do not arrive at Joe's garden as the dampened burlap is removed from the vegetables, fruit, and flowers, you may have to wait until next week for some of the best produce on the planet—that's how eager the crowds are at his Wednesday and Saturday markets. All of this is a roundabout way to say that this is Joe's favorite asparagus recipe. Simple and delectable. That's all there is to say.

1 steam asparagus until it is crisp-tender.

2 melt butter, but do not burn. Remove from heat. Sprinkle in paprika.

3 drizzle butter over cooked asparagus spears and sprinkle with Parmesan. Season as desired. Serve immediately.

baked beans with pineapple

Serves 8 to 10

1 pound adzuki beans (or red
   beans)

5 cups water

1 large onion, finely chopped

4 ounces meatless breakfast
   strips, cut up (optional;
   see note)

2 cups tomato juice

1/4 cup molasses

1 tablespoon mustard

1 tablespoon chili powder

Pepper

Salt

1 can (15 ounces) pineapple slices
   (or equivalent fresh pineapple)

Beans are a whole food that offers more protein than any other in the vegetable kingdom. They also possess complex carbohydrates and cholesterol-lowering soluble fibers.

One of the highest-quality beans is the adzuki bean. Small and dark red in color, these beans also have a pleasing taste and texture. You can generally find them at the health food store, but if you can't, red beans can be substituted.

1 cook beans in 5 cups water until tender, about 2 hours. This can be done in advance. Drain off half of the liquid.

2 sauté onions in a little water just until tender. Add breakfast strips and continue to sauté until onions are completely tender. Add remaining ingredients, except pineapple, beans, and salt, and heat until bubbly. Add beans and adjust salt at this time.

3 put beans in a large baking dish; top with sliced pineapple and some of the pineapple juice. Bake at 350 degrees F for 30 to 40 minutes.

NOTE • breakfast strips are soy-based imitation bacon. This product can be found in the freezer section of many supermarkets and health food stores alongside egg substitutes. Use 1/3 cup imitation bacon bits if you cannot find breakfast strips. If bacon bits are used, add when tomato juice is added. If you choose not to use either meatless bacon product, add a little hickory-smoked salt to create the smoky flavor.

sweet potato casserole

Serves 12

2 eggs, beaten

1 1/4 cups sugar

1 cup half-and-half

Pinch of cinnamon

Pinch of nutmeg

1 large yam or sweet potato,
    grated

2 to 3 tablespoons brandy, peach
    schnapps, or Grand Marnier

1 orange, sliced

1/4 cup butter, melted

I don't know where the original version of this holiday treat came from because it has been among friends and family for so long, with each of us customizing it along the way.

I will say that it has received enough attention that family feuds have been staged over it. There are the traditionalists who believe that sweet potatoes or yams can only be served in chunks, baked with butter and brown sugar. But the adventurous seem to prefer this recipe. It's true that holidays are about tradition, but if you slip it in now, this dish will become a tradition in another decade or two.

1 combine eggs, sugar, half-and-half, and spices and pour over grated yams in a 9 x 13 casserole dish.

2 pour liqueur over the top.

3 arrange sliced orange on top of the yams. Squeeze the juice from the ends of the oranges over the top. Pour melted butter over the top.

4 bake at 350 degrees F for about 1 hour and 30 minutes. Serve hot.

curried sweet potato pancakes

Serves 3 to 4

1 sweet potato or yam (about
   1 pound)

1 1/2 cups chopped onion

Extra-virgin olive oil

1/2 cup shredded carrots
   (optional)

2 to 3 tablespoons milk
   (or soy milk)

3/4 teaspoon curry powder

Freshly ground black pepper

1 cup cooked brown rice

Salt (or seasoned salt)

Applesauce

As a lover of potato pancakes, I created the following recipe to put some sparkle into the classic version of potato pancakes. In addition, substituting potatoes with sweet potatoes adds beta-carotene to the meal. Brown rice boosts the nutritive value even further.

1 bake or microwave yam until tender. Peel yam when cool enough to handle.

2 sauté diced onion in 1 tablespoon olive oil and a little water to keep from overheating the oil, until tender. During last couple minutes of sautéing, add carrots, if using.

3 mash up the flesh of the yam with milk as you would make mashed potatoes. Add the curry powder and pepper to taste. Add the onions–carrot mixture and rice and mix. Adjust the pepper and add salt to taste.

4 heat a nonstick skillet over medium heat. Brush the bottom of the skillet with olive oil. Drop a heaping spoonful of the potato mixture into the skillet, pressing down with the back of the spoon or spatula to form a 3-inch patty. Brown on each side and serve immediately with applesauce on the side. You should have enough "batter" to make eight 3-inch patties.

paratha

Serves 5 as a main dish, 10 as a side dish

FILLING

4 to 5 medium potatoes, baked

1 1/2 cups chopped onions and
    green onions combined

3 to 4 cloves garlic, minced or
    pressed

1 tablespoon freshly grated ginger

2 teaspoons garam masala

1 1/2 teaspoons salt

Cayenne

CHAPATI

3 cups whole wheat flour
    (see note)

1 1/2 cups water

Olive oil for sautéing

This East Indian flatbread stuffed with potatoes, onion, and classic Indian spices makes a great light meal served with yogurt and fruit.

For variety, replace potato mixture with a combination of vegetables and cheese to create your own version of paratha.

1 wash and bake potatoes, after piercing the tops a few times with a fork, until tender inside.

2 remove skins and put potatoes into a bowl. Add onions, garlic, ginger, and spices. (A fair amount of cayenne can be added, as the flavor of the potato mixture will be diluted once it is wrapped in flatbread. Go a little hotter than you normally would and it should turn out just about right.)

3 mix ingredients well with your hands and set aside.

4 to make chapati, mix flour and water together and work into a well-mixed ball with your hands. Pinch off a small lime-size piece of dough and roll out into a chapati, which is essentially an Indian version of the Mexican tortilla. Keep rolling pin and hands floured with whole wheat flour to keep the chapati from sticking.

5 pinch out an equal amount of potato mixture and place in the center of the rolled-out chapati. Fold the chapati dough over the top of the potato mixture. Pat down and roll out again into a ball about the same diameter as the first chapati you rolled out. (It will be roughly twice as thick as the plain chapati dough.)

6 cook in a heavy skillet over medium to medium-high heat in a small amount of olive oil brushed onto bottom. Serve hot. Extra parathas can be refrigerated for a few days in an airtight container with wax paper to separate them.

NOTE • the whole wheat flour used in Indian cooking is different in texture and ingredients than standard whole wheat flour. You must go to an Indian or Middle Eastern specialty store to buy the whole wheat flour ground for chapati and paratha.

focaccia with rosemary and green olives

Makes 12 slices

1 ounce dry yeast

1 1/2 tablespoons sugar

2 1/2 cups lukewarm water

2 pounds unbleached white flour
(about 7 cups)

1 tablespoon dried rosemary

1/2 cup chopped green olives

Extra-virgin olive oil

Kosher salt (or coarse sea salt)

Focaccia can be used as an accompaniment to a meal, as sandwich bread, or as the meal itself, depending on the topping. Just let your imagination fly.

1 mix yeast and sugar into water and allow yeast to dissolve.

2 put flour in a large bowl, making a well in the center. Add water mixture and begin working with hands until dough forms a ball that sticks together.

3 knead for 5 to 10 minutes, flouring your hands and the working surface to keep dough from sticking. You will know you are done kneading when the dough is smooth and no longer sticky. Sprinkle rosemary over dough and knead a couple more times until the herb is evenly distributed.

4 put dough in a lightly oiled large bowl. Let sit in a warm place and allow it to rise until it doubles in size (about 30 minutes). Rapid rising yeast can be used to speed up the process.

5 split dough in half and allow halves to rise another 20 minutes.

6 add olives by lightly kneading them into the dough. Roll out to 1/2-inch thickness and place on baking sheet coated with olive oil. Press finger or thumbprint into dough every 2 inches to create little depressions. Drizzle olive oil over the top. Sprinkle with coarse salt.

7 bake at 350 degrees F for 20 to 25 minutes. Serve hot.

VARIATION • *omit rosemary and olives and top with tomato paste, grated Asiago cheese, and black olives, or anything else you like.*

- -

RATIOS FOR REPLACING FRESH HERBS WITH DRIED • *There are recipes in which you may prefer to use dried herbs rather than fresh due to season and availability. As a simple rule of thumb: Use one-quarter the amount of dried herbs as fresh. As to the quality of taste, the debate is ongoing as chefs have their own preferences. If fresh herbs are abundant, I use them. If they are not, I'm quite happy to use dried herbs, providing they are relatively fresh. One way to assure that your dried herbs are fresh is to buy them in small amounts and replenish them more often. Some larger natural foods stores have bulk sections for herbs and spices, which is a great way to go for freshness and cost effectiveness.*

- -

lori's acorn squash

Serves 4

1 acorn squash

3 tablespoons butter

2 tablespoons brown sugar

Dash of nutmeg

A spoonful of sugar in this family favorite makes squash go down easier than ever.

1 cut squash in half and scoop out pulp and seeds.

2 dot each half with 1 1/2 tablespoons butter and 1 tablespoon brown sugar. Sprinkle with nutmeg.

3 place squash halves, skin side down, in a baking dish with 1/2 inch of water on the bottom and bake at 350 degrees F for 1 hour to 1 hour and 15 minutes. After 45 minutes, pierce the inside of the squash with a knife several times to allow flesh to be infused with butter and sugar.

4 remove from oven when tender. Cut each half in half again, making four pieces. Serve hot.

carrot–orange soufflé

Serves 4

2 cups sliced carrots

1 teaspoon freshly grated ginger

1 tablespoon orange zest

3 extra large eggs, separated

2 to 3 shakes cinnamon

1/8 to 1/4 teaspoon curry powder

Pinch of nutmeg

1/8 teaspoon salt

2 tablespoons honey

1 tablespoon butter

This slightly sweet and aromatic soufflé is a perfect accompaniment to your favorite pasta or rice entrée for entertaining.

1 heat oven to 350 degrees F.

2 steam carrots until tender but not mushy, 5 to 7 minutes.

3 purée carrots in food processor along with ginger and orange zest. Add egg yolks and purée for another 20 to 30 seconds.

4 transfer carrot mixture to bowl. Add spices, salt, and honey and stir until blended.

5 beat egg whites until they form soft peaks. Fold in carrot mixture gently until ingredients are evenly blended.

6 in the oven, heat 1 tablespoon butter in the bottom of a 1-quart baking dish for about 2 minutes, until butter is melted (see note). Pour in soufflé mixture. Bake for 25 minutes. Serve hot.

NOTE • individual baking cups can also be used. Reduce baking time by about 5 minutes.

jackie's zucchini–salsa sauté

Serves 4

1 tablespoon olive oil

1/2 cup chopped onion

1/2 cup chopped celery

2 cloves garlic, minced

1/2 cup chopped green bell pepper

2 zucchini, grated

1/2 cup salsa (medium to hot
  depending on your taste)

2 teaspoons Italian seasoning,
  or fines herbes, or herbes de
  Provence

Salt

This zesty sautéed vegetable dish can be served as a side dish or
over rice or pasta as an entrée.

1 heat olive oil over medium heat. Add onion, celery, garlic,
bell pepper, and a little water. Cook until celery begins to soften.

2 add zucchini and stir until ingredients are well mixed. Add
salsa and herbs and stir. Cover and cook over medium-low heat for
about 10 minutes. Season to taste with salt. Serve hot.

VARIATION • *serve over 6 to 8 ounces of cooked pasta
to make an entrée.*

scalloped potatoes
with leeks and chives

Serves 6

1 large leek, chopped (2 cups)

1 tablespoon extra-virgin olive oil

2 1/2 pounds potatoes, washed, peeled, and sliced

3 tablespoons butter, melted

3 tablespoons flour

Salt and pepper

1/4 cup fresh chives, chopped

1/2 cup vegetable stock

1/2 cup grated fontina cheese (or favorite cheese)

This elegant version of scalloped potatoes can be served as an entrée, in individual baking dishes, or as a side dish.

1 sauté leeks in olive oil and a little water until tender.

2 brush a small amount of oil onto bottom of 8-inch square baking dish. Divide sliced potatoes into three portions. Place one portion along bottom of baking dish. Spread half of the butter and flour over potatoes. Sprinkle with salt and pepper. Spoon half of the leeks and chives over potatoes. Repeat with next layer.

3 brush top layer of potatoes with olive oil and salt lightly. Gently pour vegetable stock over top and around edges.

4 bake at 325 degrees F for 50 minutes. Remove from oven and sprinkle cheese over top. Return to oven and continue to cook for another 10 minutes. Serve hot.

NOTE • be sure to wash the dirt out from behind the "ears" of the leeks—they hide dirt well.

baby crookneck squash

Serves 3 to 4

1/2 cup sliced green bell pepper

1 clove garlic, minced or pressed

1 large tomato, diced

1 tablespoon olive oil

2 cups sliced baby crookneck
squash

1 teaspoon fines herbes, Italian
seasoning, or herbes de
Provence

Salt

Sprinkle of sugar (if squash
is bitter)

Garden-fresh squash should be used to get the full, sweet flavor of this summertime medley. A bit of sugar can be added if the squash is on the bitter side.

1 sauté bell pepper, garlic, and tomato in oil and a little water until tender but not mushy.

2 add squash and herbs and continue to sauté until squash is crisp-tender. Salt to taste and add sugar if mixture is slightly bitter.

3 serve alone or over Spicy Rice (page 218).

east indian creamed spinach

Serves 4

1 1/3 cups diced onions

2 teaspoons olive oil

2 medium tomatoes, chopped

3 to 4 cloves garlic, minced or
   pressed

1 to 2 dashes cayenne

1/2 teaspoon garam masala
   (see note)

12 ounces fresh spinach

Salt

4 to 6 ounces Indian paneer
   cheese (or soft Buffalo
   mozzarella or tofu), cut into
   1/2-inch cubes

Garam masala, cayenne, and garlic give spinach some verve in this Indian classic also known as Palak Paneer.

1 sauté onions in olive oil and a little water over medium heat until tender. Add tomatoes and garlic and continue to sauté until tomatoes are mushy, 15 to 20 minutes, adding a little water along the way to keep the mixture from sticking to the skillet.

2 add cayenne and garam masala and stir. Add spinach and cook until the spinach is completely wilted. Season to taste with salt.

3 in a food processor, purée spinach mixture for a few seconds, leaving a little texture.

4 combine cubed cheese or tofu and spinach. Reheat in microwave or on stovetop. Serve hot.

NOTE • garam masala is an Indian spice mixture that can be found in Indian import or gourmet shops.

spicy rice

Serves 4 to 6

1 cup chopped onion

1/2 green bell pepper

1 to 2 teaspoons unrefined oil

1 clove garlic, minced

1 cup rice

1/4 teaspoon turmeric

1/8 teaspoon black pepper

Dash of cayenne

Salt

2 1/2 cups vegetable stock

This rice dish is flavorful enough that it can be served alone as a side dish, but it may be used best as a bed for a variety of vegetable dishes.

1 in a large skillet or saucepan, sauté onions and bell pepper in oil and a little water until tender. Add garlic and continue to cook for a minute. Add rice and stir.

2 add spices and stir. Add vegetable stock. Bring to a boil. Reduce heat and simmer for 30 to 35 minutes for brown rice, 20 to 25 for white rice, or until rice is tender. Serve hot.

- -

HEALTH BENEFITS OF A PLANT-BASED DIET • *Studies of the vegetarian diet have revealed the following:*

1. *Vegetarians have: lower rates of heart disease; fewer gallstones; less colon disease and lower rates of colon cancer; less lung cancer; less instances of high blood pressure; and less obesity.*

2. *Vegan diets are even healthier than lacto-ovo vegetarians.*

3. *Vegetarians consume less cholesterol.*

4. *Vegetarians consume more fiber, antioxidants (vitamin C, beta-carotene, and vitamin E), and phytochemicals.*

- -

tortes and quiches

the subject of eggs can set off some volatile discussion among vegetarians.

Some quick background: There are varying levels of vegetarians. The strictest group is the vegans. Vegans eat only from the plant kingdom. Then come the lacto-ovo vegetarians. Under this philosophy, or eating plan, a person includes foods produced by animals in his or her diet, such as milk and eggs. Someone who eats the flesh of any animal, including chicken and fish, is generally not considered vegetarian.

Most vegetarians fall into the lacto-ovo category for a variety of reasons. One primary reason is to keep their protein levels up. To eat entirely from the plant kingdom takes some education and discipline to make sure you are getting all of the nutrients needed for sustained good health and energy. Many vegetarians throw in an egg or some cottage cheese to increase their protein intake. So keep in mind that if a diet is based primarily on the plant kingdom, occasional uses of eggs and dairy are not likely to pose a health threat. Dairy also can be easily substituted with soy products.

If animal rights are important to you, you can purchase free-range or cage-free eggs. While they cost more, they do taste better—and this farming method allows the chicken to do some old-fashioned scratching around in her henhouse or in the sunlight. Happy chickens, happy eggs.

frittata mexicali

Serves 6

1 medium to large zucchini, sliced

1 medium tomato, diced

1 cup corn

1 1/2 teaspoons oregano

Seasoned salt

1/2 cup medium salsa

6 eggs, lightly beaten

Salt

1 cup grated sharp Cheddar

Dash of cayenne (optional)

Frittatas give you a great opportunity to stretch yourself and create something entirely yours. Once you have some basic ingredients in place, such as eggs and a little cheese, you can add just about anything you like. This zesty frittata is great as an entrée for brunch or a light main course for lunch or dinner.

1 sauté zucchini in a little water over medium-high heat for a minute or so. Remove zucchini from skillet before it becomes visibly soft. Add tomato and sauté for about 2 minutes, until it begins to soften.

2 add corn and continue to sauté for another minute. Add zucchini and oregano and stir. Add a little seasoned salt.

3 stir salsa into eggs. Lightly salt eggs.

4 oil the bottom and sides of a 9-inch square baking dish. Spread vegetables over the bottom of the baking dish. Place all but a small amount of the grated cheese over vegetables. Pour egg mixture over vegetables and cheese, sprinkling remaining cheese on top. Add cayenne for color if using.

5 bake at 350 degrees F for about 35 minutes, until center is firm. Serve hot.

basic pie crust

1/2 cup unsalted butter

1 cup unbleached flour or whole
   wheat pastry flour

1/4 to 1/2 teaspoon salt*

3 tablespoons water

1 cut the butter into small pieces and begin with a light touch to quickly work the butter into the flour with your hands or a fork.

2 once the butter is fairly well distributed (I prefer to quickly and lightly rub the mixture between my hands to get a very fine, cornmeal-type consistency), add salt and mix lightly. Add water and mix only until the ingredients are moistened.

3 lightly and quickly form a ball. Flour a pastry cloth or board and roll or pat into a round about 6 inches in diameter. Roll or press into pie or tart dish.

If you use salted butter you will need to reduce the amount of salt in the recipe.

notes on making your own crust • many people are intimidated about making their own crust, which is okay since there are some decent pie crusts available in the frozen food section of the supermarket. In addition, you can use a frozen puff pastry for a light and fluffy torte or quiche crust. If you want to tackle your own, however, there are a few basic rules to keep in mind:

1. Handle the dough as little as possible to get the job done. If you handle it too much, especially after the water is added, it will lose some of its flaky quality.

2. While you can pat it into the dish, it is ideal to roll it out first. You do not need to invest in a rolling pin if you don't want to. You can use a standard-size wine bottle (750 milliliters). Just remove the label and flour the bottle so it won't stick to the dough.

3. Invest in a pastry cloth. This is the best labor saving device of all when it comes to making pastry or rolling out cookies. You simply flour the surface of the cloth, roll out the dough and transfer it to the dish—no sticking. Remove the excess flour from the cloth when you are finished.

leek and mushroom frittata with brie

Serves 6

1 large leek, thoroughly cleaned
   and sliced

2 cups sliced mushrooms

1/2 fresh lemon

1/8 teaspoon salt

Pinch of nutmeg

Freshly grated black pepper

2 eggs

2 egg yolks

1/2 cup whole milk

1/2 cup half-and-half

2/3 cup grated aged Gouda

2 ounces Brie, cut into small
   pieces

This elegant frittata derives much of its flavor from the leeks. The national emblem of Wales, leeks resemble oversized scallions but have a milder taste. Combine the sautéed leeks with a little Brie cheese and you have a truly gourmet frittata. And, while it may sound a little fancy, all of the ingredients should be available at a good supermarket.

When cooking with leeks, be sure to split them lengthwise and wash them well as they have lots of dirt behind their little ears and under their fingernails.

1 sauté leek and mushrooms in a little water until very tender, sprinkling with fresh lemon juice while cooking. Add salt, nutmeg, and pepper to taste. Mix well.

2 beat eggs, egg yolks, milk, and half-and-half with a whisk until well blended.

3 lightly oil the bottom of a pie plate or 9-inch square baking dish.

4 place mushroom mixture on bottom of baking dish. Sprinkle Gouda and Brie on top of vegetables. Pour egg mixture over the top, stirring with a fork lightly here and there to keep vegetables and cheese evenly distributed.

5 bake at 375 degrees F for 25 to 30 minutes. Serve hot or at room temperature.

GROWING A WINDOW HERB GARDEN • *Growing your own herbs indoors is easier than you think and can be really rewarding in the chilly winter months. All you need is a windowsill that gets a good amount of light. One thing to keep in mind is that because windowsills only allow for small pots, you'll need to water then often. If you are forgetful or travel, you might consider using plastic or glazed ceramic pots to hold in the moisture. I learned this the hard way by planting in the classic terra cotta pots, leaving town, and returning to a virtual dried herb garden.*

Here are some herbs that cut you a little slack on upkeep: marjoram, oregano, basil (it wilts easily, but comes back to life quickly with a little water), rosemary, thyme, mint, sage, and tarragon. I found chives to be somewhat delicate and temperamental as well as parsley. This is likely my own fault. Nonetheless, the others survived.

----

polenta torte

Serves 6

2 1/2 cups water

1 1/2 cups polenta

1/4 teaspoon salt

3/4 cup grated Cheddar, fontina, or
   Gouda cheese

3 cups mushrooms, sliced

1 onion, thinly sliced

2 teaspoons extra-virgin olive oil

1/4 cup red wine

1 large zucchini, julienned

1/4 teaspoon herbes de Provence
   (or Italian seasoning)

Salt

Polenta is relatively new on the torte scene. In this recipe, herbs, onion, red wine, and cheese give the neutral polenta a full flavor.

1 boil water and add polenta and salt. Cook for a short time over medium heat until polenta has thickened, making sure it is not too thick to spread into the pan. Mix cheese into polenta and stir until the cheese has melted.

2 sauté the mushrooms and onions in oil and red wine over medium heat until the mushrooms are wilted and moist, but not all of the moisture has evaporated. Add the zucchini and continue to cook until the zucchini begins to soften but is not soggy. Season with herbes de Provence and salt to taste. Remove vegetables from heat.

3 spread half of the polenta onto the bottom of a lightly oiled 8-inch torte pan. Top with the vegetable mixture. Spread remaining half of polenta on top of vegetables.

4 bake at 375 degrees F for about 25 minutes, or until heated through.

NOTE • to julienne a vegetable is to cut it into thin, matchstick pieces.

swiss chard torte

Serves 8

1 (9-inch) pie crust (see note)

1/3 cup chopped onion

1 cup chopped leeks

2 cloves garlic, minced or pressed

1 tablespoon extra-virgin olive oil

Pinch of nutmeg

1/4 teaspoon savory salt

Freshly ground black pepper

8 cups chopped, cleaned Swiss
   chard

1 1/4 cups grated Gruyère cheese

2 eggs, beaten

When selecting chard for the following dish, be sure the stalks of the leaves are turgid and the leaves a fresh green with no yellow spots. Like spinach, chard is full of vitamins A and C, plus iron, calcium, magnesium, and potassium. Combine it with leeks, garlic, and Gruyère cheese and you have a wonderful tasting torte.

1 heat oven to 400 degrees F. Bake pie shell for 6 to 7 minutes and remove from oven.

2 sauté onion, leeks, and garlic in olive oil and a little water until tender. Add nutmeg, savory salt, and pepper to taste and stir.

3 toss in Swiss chard and cook for about 1 minute, until chard begins to wilt and reduce in size, without cooking it all the way down. Remove from heat.

4 spoon chard mixture over bottom of pie crust. Sprinkle 1 cup of the cheese over the chard mixture. Pour eggs over chard and cheese evenly and slowly. Sprinkle remaining cheese on top and bake at 400 degrees F for 20 to 25 minutes. Serve hot or at room temperature.

NOTE • I have always made pie crusts from scratch (see page 225, but when I'm in a hurry, Pet Ritz–brand pie shells work well for tortes.

asparagus–mushroom quiche

Serves 6 to 8

1 (9-inch) pie shell

1 cup fresh asparagus, cut up

1 cup sliced mushrooms

1 tablespoon butter

3 to 4 tablespoons white wine

White and black pepper

Salt

Pinch of nutmeg (optional)

4 eggs

2 cups whole milk

6 ounces Gruyère cheese, grated

How can you go wrong with Gruyère cheese and asparagus as the key components of a quiche?

Now widely copied by many countries, Gruyère was and still is a product of the Swiss. Named after the village of its origins, it is still made in the mountainous region and bears a somewhat sweet and slightly nutty flavor, making it ideal as both a table cheese and for cooking.

1 heat oven to 400 degrees F. Bake pie shell for 6 to 7 minutes and remove from oven.

2 sauté asparagus and mushrooms in butter and a little water over medium heat. Add wine, white and black peppers, and salt to taste. Add nutmeg if using. Continue to sauté until vegetables begin to soften to a crisp-tender texture, making sure not to overcook. Remove from heat.

3 c o m b i n e eggs and milk in a bowl and beat until smooth. You may add a little salt at this time, but not much because the Gruyère cheese is salty. Adjust pepper at this time.

4 s p r i n k l e grated cheese over the bottom of the pie crust. Spoon vegetables over the cheese. Pour egg mixture over cheese and vegetables.

5 r e d u c e oven temperature to 375 degrees F and bake for 35 to 40 minutes. Cool for about 15 minutes before serving.

garden torte

Serves 6 to 8

1 (9-inch) pie crust

1 small eggplant, peeled and sliced
   in 1/4-inch-thick slices

2 yellow zucchini (or 3 crookneck
   squash), sliced

1 large potato, peeled and sliced in
   1/4-inch-thick slices

1 red bell pepper, cut in half
   lengthwise

Extra-virgin olive oil

Salt and freshly ground black pepper

5 medium tomatoes, chopped

Italian seasoning or fines herbes
   (basil, rosemary, thyme, etc.)

Cinnamon

Dash of cayenne

4 ounces fontina cheese, grated

This torte derives its exquisite flavor from a native Italian cheese—fontina. This distinctive tasting cheese was the gentry's choice as early as the thirteenth century. When it reaches a more mature state, the firmer and drier texture is ideal for grating and using as a condiment.

There is also a Danish version of fontina that can be used in this recipe. The Danish cheese is more commonly found in supermarkets, whereas you may have to go to a gourmet shop or cheese store to find the Italian variety.

1 heat oven to 400 degrees F. Bake pie shell for 6 to 7 minutes and remove from oven.

2 place all sliced vegetables except tomatoes on 2 lightly oiled cookie sheets. Brush vegetables very lightly with olive oil. Lightly sprinkle with salt and pepper. Bake for 20 minutes.

3 while vegetables are baking, sauté tomatoes in 1 to 2 table-spoons olive oil over medium-high heat. Sprinkle Italian seasonings, cinnamon, and cayenne over tomatoes while they are cooking, waiting until the end to add salt. Cook tomatoes until most, but not all, of the moisture is gone. Taste and adjust the spices to your liking.

4 when vegetables are done roasting, cut red peppers into strips. Layer vegetables in pie crust, spreading tomato sauce over vegetables every two layers. In the middle of layering, sprinkle half of the cheese. Top with remaining grated cheese. Bake at 350 degrees F for 20 to 25 minutes. Serve hot.

feta and sun-dried tomato frittata

Serves 3 to 4

1 clove garlic, finely chopped

1/3 to 1/2 cup chopped sun-dried
   tomatoes

2 teaspoons extra virgin olive oil

1/3 cup chopped parsley

1/3 cup chopped fresh basil

2 pinches thyme

Salt and pepper

6 eggs, lightly beaten

1/2 cup crumbled feta cheese

Feta and the sun-drenched hearty flavor of sun-dried tomatoes make for a full-flavored frittata that can be served at any time of the day. Try to use fresh basil if at all possible to get the full aromatic power of the herb.

1 quickly sauté garlic and sun-dried tomatoes in a little water for a couple minutes. Add oil, parsley, and basil, toss. (Soften dehydrated tomatoes before sautéing by boiling them for a few minutes.) Remove from heat.

2 add thyme, salt, and pepper. In a bowl, combine the sautéed mixture and eggs and mix.

3 pour egg mixture into a medium-size ovenproof skillet lightly coated with olive oil. Sprinkle feta cheese over the top. Cover and cook on medium-low heat until bottom and sides of egg mixture solidify. To firm up the top of the eggs, place under the broiler for a minute or so, watching carefully. Remove when eggs are firm and serve immediately.

NOTE • wait until just before using to chop or tear the basil, which loses some of its essential oils if the bruised or cut leaves are left exposed to air.

soy dishes

tofu and broccoli in peanut sauce

honey-mustard tofu salad

tempeh con queso

mexican tofu

chilled lemon–rice soup

faux beef spaghetti sauce

spanish rice with tempeh

stuffed peppers with tempeh and rice

not-so-sloppy joes

tempeh tacos

barbecue tofu with caramelized onions

lentil loaf

teriyaki eggplant and tofu

tofu and broccoli in peanut sauce

Serves 4

8 ounces firm, Chinese-style tofu

2 tablespoons peanut oil

2 to 3 tablespoons water

1 tablespoon shoyu

2 cups broccoli florets, cut into
small pieces

1/2 teaspoon finely minced fresh
ginger

2 tablespoons finely chopped onion

2 tablespoons peanut butter

1/2 cup soy milk

2 tablespoons water

1 1/2 teaspoons freshly squeezed
lemon juice

1/2 teaspoon vinegar

Dash of cayenne or chile oil
(optional)

2 to 3 tablespoons chopped
peanuts (for garnish)

This recipe was influenced by Thai dishes I've enjoyed in the many Thai restaurants on the West Coast. This tangy, peanutty tofu dish can be served as a side dish or over noodles or rice for a filling main course.

1 in skillet or wok, quickly sauté tofu over medium-high heat in 1 tablespoon peanut oil, water, and 1/2 teaspoon shoyu for 2 minutes. Remove from skillet.

2 add 1/2 tablespoon peanut oil and a little water to hot skillet and heat for a moment. Add broccoli and 1/2 teaspoon shoyu. Cook until broccoli just begins to soften (1 to 2 minutes) and remove from skillet.

3 heat remaining 1/2 tablespoon peanut oil and a little water. Add ginger and onion and sauté until onion is tender.

4 add peanut butter and stir (mixture will be thick and sticky). Add soy milk slowly, stirring until you reach a creamy texture. If the sauce is too thick, slowly begin adding water until sauce reaches desired consistency.

5 add lemon juice, vinegar, and the remaining 2 teaspoons shoyu and stir. Make any adjustments in flavoring at this time, including the addition of cayenne or chile oil.

6 add tofu and broccoli to sauce and mix well. Serve as a side dish or over noodles or rice. Garnish with chopped peanuts.

honey-mustard tofu salad

Serves 4

14 ounces extra-firm tofu, cut into
    small cubes

1 to 2 tablespoons fresh unrefined
    oil

3 tablespoons water

1 tablespoon ground mustard seed

1 tablespoon prepared mustard

2 tablespoons honey

1 tablespoon shoyu (or soy sauce)

1 clove garlic, minced or pressed

4 servings cleaned, torn lettuce

4 slices onion, rings separated

1/3 cup roasted peanuts

1/4 to 1/3 cup Basic Vinaigrette
    (page 57)

Here's a sweet and tangy way for you to incorporate tofu into your diet. Peanuts combine with soy to boost the protein level of this dish.

1 sauté tofu in oil and water over medium-high heat, stirring regularly until all sides of cubes are cooked 7 to 8 minutes.

2 mix together ground mustard seed, prepared mustard, honey, shoyu, and garlic. Add to tofu and cook for a minute or so, tossing. Remove from heat.

3 place lettuce on individual plates. Place onion slices on lettuce, followed by tofu sauté and peanuts. Drizzle dressing over the top. Serve warm or cold.

tempeh con queso

Serves 10

1 1/2 packages (12 ounces total)
    frozen tempeh

4 green onions, finely chopped

3 tablespoons butter
    (or margarine)

1 can (4 ounces) diced green
    chiles

1 can (2 1/4 ounces) chopped
    olives

1 can (8 ounces) tomato sauce

1/2 to 1 cup water

12 ounces sharp Cheddar cheese,
    grated

1 to 3 teaspoons Worcestershire
    sauce

1 bag (12 ounces) tortilla chips

The original version of this recipe was Chile con Queso, using ground beef in the place of tempeh. The dish has lost nothing in the translation except the fat and toughness of the beef. Do keep in mind, however, that this is more or less a party dish, to be consumed on special occasions, because of the large amount of cheese used. Lowfat and nonfat cheeses are also an option.

1 thaw tempeh. Break into bits and sauté, along with green onions, in butter until lightly browned.

2 add green chiles, olives, tomato sauce, and 1/2 cup water and continue to cook until bubbly. Add cheese, sprinkling in a little at a time, stirring constantly. Add Worcestershire sauce, tasting for the desired amount. If mixture becomes too thick, add a little more water. Serve immediately in chafing dish with tortilla chips.

mexican tofu

Serves 4

1 cup rice

1 tablespoon oil

1 large ear of corn

1 cup thinly sliced onion

2/3 cup chopped green bell pepper

1 pound firm tofu, cut into cubes

1 tablespoon shoyu

1/2 cup mole sauce

The flavor in this dish comes from the mole sauce, which you can find in the Mexican food section of the supermarket.

Serving the tofu over rice makes a nutritiously solid, warm entrée, but I also like this tofu refrigerated and served on its own. I eat it in little portions at a time when I need a protein pickup.

1 begin cooking rice according to package directions.

2 heat oil and a little water in a large skillet over medium-high heat. Sauté corn, onion, and bell pepper until onion is tender. Remove vegetables from skillet and set aside.

3 in the same skillet, over medium-high heat, begin cooking tofu cubes, sprinkling shoyu over them as they cook. After 1 to 2 minutes, add mole sauce. Continue to cook until the sauce begins to stick to the tofu and the tofu begins to firm up on the outside. Add vegetables. Stir and continue to cook for another minute or so. Serve hot over a portion of rice.

NOTE • this dish is also good on its own, cold or hot. You may want to add more mole sauce when serving over rice. Worcestershire sauce, chili powder, and soy sauce can all be used to adjust the flavor of the mole sauce to your liking.

chilled lemon–rice soup

Serves 4

1/2 cup rice

2 cups chopped fresh spinach

3 to 3 1/2 tablespoons shoyu
   (or soy sauce)

6 ounces firm tofu, cut into small
   cubes

4 cups vegetable stock

Juice of 1/2 lemon

Dash of cayenne

4 to 5 ice cubes or (1/2 cup
   cold water)

This soup is a refreshing, cool summer soup, but can also be eaten warm in cold weather.

1 boil or steam the rice until it reaches desired level of doneness, rinse with cold water, and set aside.

2 if you have a steamer, put spinach inside and place it over the cooking rice for 1 minute. This will slightly wilt the spinach without overcooking it.

3 heat skillet over medium-high heat. Add 1 1/2 to 2 tablespoons shoyu and tofu cubes. Sauté for a couple of minutes, stirring constantly, until the moisture has been steamed out of tofu. Remove from heat.

4 put vegetable stock in a bowl or saucepan. Add lemon juice and 1 1/2 tablespoons shoyu. Sprinkle lightly with cayenne. Add cooked rice, tofu, and spinach. For chilled soup, add ice cubes, stir until melted, and serve. For hot soup, heat in saucepan or microwave.

faux beef spaghetti sauce

Serves 8 to 10

1 large onion, diced

1 green bell pepper, diced

4 stalks celery, sliced

1 pound mushrooms, sliced

1 to 2 cloves garlic, finely chopped

1/4 cup extra-virgin olive oil

1 large can (28 ounces) tomatoes

3 cups tomato sauce

1 cup beef- or chicken-flavored
   TVP (optional)

3/4 teaspoon basil

1/2 teaspoon oregano

Parsley

Salt and pepper

Savory salt

1 tablespoon sugar

3 cups water

TVP sounds like it should be an industrial solvent. In fact, it stands for texturized vegetable protein, which is a soy-based meat substitute. Beef-flavored TVP can be deceptively similar to ground beef when used in a sauce such as this one. These products are particularly appealing to those who are trying to eliminate red meat from the diet but still enjoy the flavor and texture of ground beef.

1 in a large saucepan, sauté onions, bell pepper, celery, mushrooms, and garlic in oil and a little water until slightly tender.

2 add all other ingredients and simmer for about 4 hours. Add water as needed if mixture becomes too thick or dry. Serve over pasta with a little freshly grated Parmesan or Romano cheese.

spanish rice with tempeh

Serves 6 to 8

1 medium onion, chopped

1 small green bell pepper, chopped

2 tablespoons extra-virgin olive oil

1 cup long-grain rice (preferably basmati)

1 rounded tablespoon spicy mustard

1 can (8 ounces) tomato sauce

Salt

2 cups water

Freshly ground black pepper

1 package (10 ounces) tempeh

2 tablespoons extra-virgin olive oil

1/2 small packet taco seasoning

2/3 to 3/4 cup water

This simple Spanish rice recipe has been one of our favorite rice dishes since we were kids. Mom's secret was mustard, which gives it a distinctive twist.

1 sauté the onions and bell pepper in oil and a little water over medium heat until tender.

2 add rice and stir for a minute. Add mustard and stir. Add tomato sauce, salt, and water. Sprinkle generous amounts of pepper to give it a little heat. Bring to a boil. Reduce heat and simmer, covered, for another 20 to 25 minutes. Add more water along the way if necessary.

3 remove from heat when rice reaches desired level of doneness.

4 sauté tempeh, crumbled into little bits, in oil and half of the water until water is absorbed. Sprinkle taco seasonings over tempeh, tossing until tempeh is coated. Add other half of the water to tempeh to plump it up. When water is absorbed continue cooking for another minute.

5 add tempeh to cooked rice, mix thoroughly, reheat, and serve.

VARIATION • *this dish can also be made without the tempeh and is wonderful for use in burritos or as a side dish.*

stuffed peppers with tempeh and rice

Serves 4

4 medium green bell peppers

2/3 cup mixed rice

4 ounces tempeh, crumbled

3 tablespoons extra-virgin olive oil

Seasoned salt

1/4 cup water

2/3 cup chopped onion

1 to 2 cloves garlic, chopped

1 medium tomato, diced

2 tablespoons finely chopped soft-
    ened sun-dried tomatoes

1 tablespoon capers

1/4 teaspoon thyme

Freshly ground black pepper

You won't miss the meat in this tempeh-based recipe, which has all of the flavor of many meat-based versions you may have enjoyed. Though the ingredients list is on the long side, most are common items you are likely to have on hand.

1 cut tops off bell peppers and remove seeds. Place in boiling water and remove from heat. Let stand immersed for 10 minutes to soften peppers. Remove from water and set aside.

2 cook rice until tender according to package directions. Set aside.

3 sauté tempeh in 1 tablespoon oil over medium heat until lightly browned, lightly sprinkling with seasoned salt. Add water and allow it to be absorbed, which will take about 30 seconds. Set aside.

4 sauté chopped onion and garlic in 1 tablespoon oil and a little water over medium heat until onions begin to soften. Add fresh tomato, sun-dried tomatoes, capers, thyme, and pepper to taste and continue to cook for another 5 minutes.

5 add rice and tempeh to vegetables, heat for a minute, and adjust salt and pepper.

6 scoop into peppers and bake at 350 degrees F for about 20 minutes. Serve hot.

VITAMIN B-12 IN THE DIET • *One common concern among vegetarians is about the level of vitamin B-12 in a meatless diet since the largest supply of B-12 comes from animal proteins. It is available in non-meat sources such as ricotta cheese made from the whey produced from mozzarella and provolone. Ricotta contains a rich supply of B vitamins including B-12.*

For a non-dairy source, tempeh offers B-12. Though much of the B-12 in tempeh has been destroyed through the newer, sterile methods of production, some manufacturers now inject friendly bacteria that cultivates the growth of B-12 into the soybeans to restore B-12 levels. Algae and yeasts also contain rich sources of B-12.

Since B-12 is important for the nervous system and red blood cell production, it is also an option to take B-12 supplements if you show signs of B-12 deficiency.

----

not-so-sloppy joes

Serves 6

2/3 cup chopped onion

2/3 cup chopped green bell pepper

2 tablespoons extra-virgin olive oil

2 tempeh patties (8 ounces each),
    thawed and crumbled

1 cup water

1 1/2 tablespoons molasses

1 to 2 tablespoons brown sugar

1 can (15 ounces) tomato sauce

4 to 6 tablespoons hickory smoke-
    flavor barbecue sauce

1 to 2 tablespoons vinegar

1 teaspoon Worcestershire sauce

6 hamburger-style buns

As kids, Sloppy Joes were always one of our favorite taste treats—when we could get Mom to make them. Sadly, I let them go when I became a vegetarian, but, as with many recipes in this book, I found a way to create the same taste experience without the use of meat. This, by the way, is a popular dish with kids.

1 sauté onion and bell pepper in oil and a little water for 1 to 2 minutes. Add crumbled tempeh and water and continue to cook until tempeh has absorbed all the water.

2 add the remaining ingredients, except buns, tasting as you go to reach the desired balance of sweet and tart. Simmer for 5 to 10 minutes, adding more water when necessary to keep a moist but not watery texture.

3 spoon a portion of mixture over halves of heated hamburger buns and serve.

VARIATION • *although not-so-sloppy joes are good on their own, you can make a sandwich out of them by adding mayonnaise, lettuce, and tomatoes.*

tempeh tacos

Serves 6

2 packages (8 ounces each) frozen
    tempeh

1/2 cup water

1 packet taco seasoning (or your
    favorite taco seasonings)

2 tablespoons fresh unrefined oil

12 corn tortillas (or packaged taco
    shells)

1/2 pound Cheddar or Jack cheese,
    grated

Diced tomatoes

Chopped or shredded lettuce

Diced avocado

Taco sauce (optional)

If this one doesn't work with the kids and brother-in-law, I don't know what will. With none of the cholesterol, fat, and gristle of hamburger, tempeh provides the protein and bulk in this homey taco recipe. Always a crowd pleaser.

1 thaw tempeh. Break apart into bits the size of browned hamburger pieces.

2 sauté tempeh in water, taco seasoning, and oil until water is absorbed. Turn heat to low to keep warm.

3 prepare taco shells by placing them on a plate with damp paper towels between each tortilla. Microwave covered in plastic wrap for about 30 to 60 seconds, until tortillas are hot. If you don't have a microwave, cover with aluminum foil and place in a hot oven for about 5 minutes.

4 assemble tacos by layering tempeh mixture in taco shells, followed by cheese and your choice of remaining ingredients.

barbecue tofu with caramelized onions

Serves 4

1 pound onions, thinly sliced

2 tablespoons butter

1 tablespoon oil

12 ounces firm tofu, sliced in
   1/4-inch strips

2/3 cup spicy barbecue sauce

8 slices of bread (or 4 hamburger buns)

1 large tomato, thinly sliced

8 lettuce leaves

How can you go wrong with barbecue sauce and caramelized onions? The beauty of tofu is that it takes on all of the flavors of the food it's combined with.

1 in a skillet, sauté sliced onions in butter over medium-high heat until very brown, even slightly scorched in places.

2 at the same time, brush the bottom of another skillet with oil, and heat over a medium heat. Coat tofu strips with barbecue sauce, place each strip in the heated skillet, and allow to cook until the bottom side looks slightly charred. Turn each strip over and cook until slightly charred on other side.

3 keep tofu and onions warm while cooking second batch of tofu if the pan is not large enough to accommodate all slices.

4 place strips of tofu and generous portions of onions on toasted or soft bread, along with tomatoes, lettuce, and any other sandwich condiments you enjoy. Serve immediately.

lentil loaf

Serves 6 to 8

1 3/4 cups chopped onion

1 clove garlic, minced

6 ounces tempeh, broken into bits

2 tablespoons extra-virgin olive oil

1 cup shredded carrots

1 cup shredded apples

Freshly ground pepper

2 1/2 cups cooked lentils

1 cup bread crumbs

1 1/4 cups grated Cheddar cheese

1/2 to 3/4 teaspoon seasoned salt

2 eggs, beaten

1/3 cup liquid (vegetable stock or
water)

Lentil Loaf is a popular way for vegetarians to get a balanced meal and can be used in any way in which meat loaf would be used. Apples and Cheddar cheese give this version a rich, slightly sweet flavor.

1 sauté onions, garlic, and tempeh in oil and a little water until onions begin to soften.

2 add carrots and apples and continue to sauté until all vegetables are soft. Sprinkle a generous amount of pepper on mixture.

3 add lentils, bread crumbs, cheese, and seasoned salt and mix. Adjust salt at this time. Add eggs and liquid and mix well. Put mixture into lightly oiled loaf pan. Bake at 350 degrees F for 45 minutes.

VARIATIONS • *curry loaf: add 1 to 2 teaspoons curry powder; Italian loaf: add 1 teaspoon mixed Italian seasonings; Herb loaf: add 2 teaspoons ground rubbed sage; All-American: add 8 ounces corn to loaf mixture and ketchup on top; and French loaf: add 1/2 teaspoon each rosemary and tarragon.*

teriyaki eggplant and tofu

Serves 6

1 cup rice

2 medium eggplants, sliced, cut into quarters, and salted

1 large onion, sliced and quartered

1 large red bell pepper, chopped

1 to 2 tablespoons extra-virgin olive oil

1/2 cup Gourmet Teriyaki Sauce (page 52)

8 ounces extra-firm tofu, sliced into 1/4-inch-thick strips

Freshly ground black pepper

Gourmet Teriyaki Sauce can make just about any tofu or vegetable dish special.

1 cook rice according to package directions. Rinse salt from eggplant.

2 sauté eggplant, onion, and bell pepper in oil and a little water over medium-high heat. Add 2/3 of the teriyaki sauce and black pepper to taste to the vegetables and continue to sauté until eggplant is soft and moisture is reduced. Remove from heat and set aside.

3 brush bottom of skillet with a very small amount of oil to prevent sticking, and heat over medium heat.

4 brush or dip tofu strips in teriyaki sauce, sprinkle pepper on lightly, and sauté until slightly browned and firm on each side. Quickly reheat vegetables.

5 serve vegetables over rice, placing strips of tofu on top.

sandwiches, pizza, and more

spicy white bean burritos

vegurritos (vegetarian burritos)

barbecued eggplant sandwich

barbecue vegetable pita

garden burgers

spicy artichoke heart fajitas

broccoli–spinach pizza

curried eggplant and peppers sandwich

grilled garden sandwich

vegetarian reuben sandwich

spicy white bean burritos

Serves 4

BEAN MIXTURE

1 can (15 ounces) white beans,
   drained and rinsed

3 tablespoons freshly squeezed
   lemon juice

1 tablespoon sesame tahini

2 teaspoons finely chopped
   jalapeño pepper

1/4 heaping teaspoon ground
   cumin

1 large clove garlic (or 2 small
   cloves), pressed or minced

1/4 teaspoon salt

Dash of cayenne

Sliced fontina cheese

4 large flour tortillas

Thinly sliced red onion

Sliced tomatoes

Salsa

A little bit of tahini goes a long way. It is this Middle Eastern cooking staple that gives this burrito its rich and distinct flavor. In fact, it's hard to return to your basic refried bean burritos after experiencing this taste treat.

1 place all of the bean mixture ingredients in a food processor and blend until smooth.

2 brush skillet with a little oil and heat over medium heat. Do not allow oil to burn (smoke).

3 place cheese slices in center of each tortilla. Top with 1/4 cup bean mixture. Top with onion, tomato, and salsa. Fold like an envelope and heat each burrito in skillet until cheese begins to melt. Serve hot.

NOTE • while this recipe uses the bean paste as a burrito filling, it also stands well on its own as a dip. A good pairing would be flatbread or Amaranth crackers.

vegurritos (vegetarian burritos)

Serves 10

SPANISH RICE

1 onion, chopped

2/3 bell pepper, chopped

2 tablespoons extra-virgin olive oil

1 1/4 cups rice (preferably basmati)

1 to 2 tablespoons mustard

1 can (8 ounces) tomato sauce

2 1/2 cups water

Salt and pepper

PINTO BEANS

2 quarts water

1/2 pound pinto beans

2 to 3 tablespoons imitation bacon bits

1/2 to 1 teaspoon ground cumin

2 tablespoons unrefined oil

Salt

1/2 pound Monterey Jack, sharp
  Cheddar, or Gouda, grated

Cooked kernel corn

Salsa

10 burrito-size tortillas

Sour cream

Chopped tomatoes

These burritos take some time to prepare because everything is made from scratch except the tortillas. As long as you're going to all this trouble, it's a good idea to make a big batch and freeze them in a microwave-safe wrapping.

1 to make the Spanish rice, sauté onion and bell pepper in extra-virgin olive oil and a little water until tender. Stir in rice. Add mustard and stir. Add all other ingredients and bring to a boil. Lower heat and simmer, covered, for 20 to 25 minutes. Check rice after 15 minutes to see if more water is needed.

2 to make the pinto beans, heat water in pot. Add all other ingredients and simmer for 2 to 3 hours, checking occasionally to see if more water is needed.

3 place rice, then beans, cheese, corn, and salsa into center of each tortilla. Fold in ends and roll or fold.

4 wrap individually in foil first, and bake at 350 degrees F for about 15 minutes until heated. You can also wrap in plastic wrap and microwave for 1 to 2 minutes. Serve with sour cream, tomatoes, and more salsa on side.

barbecued eggplant sandwich

Serves 4

1 red bell pepper

Olive oil

1 eggplant, peeled and sliced in
   1/4-inch-thick rounds

1/3 cup spicy barbecue sauce

Salt and pepper

8 large slices of sourdough bread

4 ounces fontina cheese, thinly
   sliced, optional

2 medium tomatoes, sliced

8 lettuce leaves

Mayonnaise (optional)

This sandwich offers a refreshing change for backyard parties. Since eggplant is the main ingredient and essentially neutral in flavor, it's best to find a quality barbecue sauce to carry the taste of the sandwich.

1 prepare charcoals. Cut red pepper in half, remove seeds, and lightly coat with olive oil inside and out.

2 place red peppers and eggplant slices on grill, brushing both sides of eggplant with barbecue sauce. Lightly salt and pepper. Barbecue until soft. Cut red peppers into strips.

3 after eggplant is cooked, place sourdough bread on grill, and put cheese slices on half of the pieces. Cook until toasted on one side only. Remove from barbecue.

4 to assemble sandwiches, place 2 to 3 slices of eggplant on bread, followed by sliced red peppers, tomato, and lettuce. Garnish with mayonnaise or more barbecue sauce if desired.

barbecue vegetable pita

Serves 4

4 pita pockets (wheat or white)

2 carrots, thinly sliced

1/2 head cauliflower, chopped

1 1/2 cups mushrooms, sliced

1 green bell pepper, diced

3 tablespoons oil

1 to 2 yellow crookneck squash,
   sliced

3 to 4 tablespoons barbecue sauce

Salt and pepper

4 to 6 ounces Monterey Jack,
   Cheddar, or fontina cheese,
   grated, optional

This recipe combines a touch of the Middle East with the Southwest to produce an interesting "meal in a pocket." While it may not be the barbecue you were used to as a kid growing up in Texas or Louisiana, it's a lot better for you than a side of ribs.

1 cut the pita bread in half, cover, and warm in the oven or microwave.

2 sauté carrots, cauliflower, mushrooms, and peppers in oil and a little water for 3 to 4 minutes, stirring. Add squash and continue to cook for another few minutes until squash and other vegetables begin to soften when pierced with a fork. Do not overcook. Add barbecue sauce, salt, and pepper and stir until vegetables are coated. Remove from heat.

3 remove pita pockets from oven. Sprinkle grated cheese in each half, followed by vegetables. Serve immediately.

VARIATION • *cashews can be added when assembling the pockets for additional flavor and texture.*

garden burgers

Serves 6 to 8

1 cup shredded carrots

1 1/2 cups finely chopped
  mushrooms

1/2 cup chopped green onions

Unrefined oil

2 cups cooked brown rice

1 cup grated Cheddar cheese

1/2 cup cottage cheese (optional)

Vega-sal, Spike, or favorite brand
  seasoned salt

Curry powder (optional)

1 1/2 tablespoons whole wheat or
  white flour

1 egg, beaten

1 to 2 tablespoons extra-virgin
  olive oil

You may have noticed a new addition to burger menus around the country—garden burgers, sometimes called veggie burgers. Interestingly, they often cost as much as or more than beef hamburgers despite the fact that the ingredients cost just pennies. The remedy? Make them at home. Not only are they inexpensive to make, these Garden Burgers taste better than most found in restaurants or stores.

1 in a nonstick skillet or saucepan, sauté carrots, mushrooms, and green onions in a very small amount of unrefined oil and a little water to keep oil from overheating. Remove from heat.

2 add vegetables to cooked brown rice and stir. Add cheese, cottage cheese, seasoned salt to taste, and curry powder (if using) and stir.

3 stir flour into beaten egg. Add to rice and vegetable mixture.

4 form mixture into patties with your hands and drop directly into nonstick skillet brushed with oil. Patties are very fragile in an uncooked state, so handle them carefully.

5 cook over medium heat for a few minutes on each side, until the patties turn slightly golden. Serve immediately, or freeze for future use, making sure to wrap them well to protect against freezer burn.

VARIATION • *for variety use barbecue sauce, teriyaki sauce, curried mayonnaise, or plain mustard and ketchup along with fresh tomatoes, lettuce, avocados, sprouts, onions, and other toppings to complete your garden burger.*

spicy artichoke heart fajitas

Serves 8

1 large onion, sliced and quartered

1 can (7 ounces) whole green
   chiles, sliced in 1/2-inch strips

1 jar (6 ounces) artichoke hearts,
   sliced in quarters

8 medium flour tortillas

1 1/3 cups cooked rice (boiled in
   vegetable broth)

2/3 cup Gouda or Edam cheese,
   grated

1/2 cup sour cream

1/2 cup salsa

Chiles, artichoke hearts, and salsa make this fajita recipe anything but bland. Some who have been served this fajita say it's the best they've had. Try it for yourself and see what you think.

1 sauté the onions and chiles together until the onions become tender. Add a little water if necessary. Add artichoke hearts and continue to sauté until artichokes are hot.

2 in oven or microwave, warm tortillas, wrapped in foil or plastic to retain moisture.

3 layer rice, artichoke heart mixture, cheese, sour cream, and salsa on warm tortilla. Roll up and serve immediately.

broccoli–spinach pizza

Serves 4 to 6

2 cups broccoli florets

1 to 2 cloves garlic, finely chopped

2 tablespoons olive oil

Fresh lemon juice

Salt

Freshly grated black pepper

1 bunch fresh spinach, washed and
   dried

1 (12-inch) pizza crust (homemade, Boboli, etc.; see note)

1/2 cup grated mozzarella

1/2 cup grated fontina (Jack,
   Cheddar, provolone, even feta
   can be used)

Parmesan cheese, grated

Crushed red peppers (optional)

It used to be that salami and pepperoni were the only obvious
choices for pizza toppings. Fortunately, there is no limit these days
to what you can pile on top of this international favorite.

Though it may sound a bit too healthy, I guarantee that if you are a
spinach and broccoli fan, this pizza will win you over.

1 sauté the broccoli and garlic in olive oil and a little water for
just a few minutes, leaving the broccoli partially crunchy. Squeeze
a little lemon juice over broccoli while sautéing. Add salt and pepper to taste. Remove from burner.

2 toss fresh spinach in with sautéed broccoli.

3 spread broccoli and spinach out over pizza crust. Sprinkle
grated cheeses over vegetables. Top with a dusting of Parmesan
cheese. Sprinkle a little more black pepper on top. Bake at 450
degrees F until bubbly. Serve immediately with crushed red pepper
sprinkled on top.

NOTE • I gave up making my own pizza crust when
I found Boboli. It has a great flavor and texture and can be
found at most supermarkets. The only drawback is its price of
about $3.29 for a 12-inch crust. Keep in mind that if you use
a Boboli crust you only need to cook the pizza for 6 to 7 minutes. For homemade crust, lower the oven temperature a bit
and cook for 15 to 20 minutes.

curried eggplant
and peppers sandwich

Serves 5 to 6

Salt

1 eggplant, cubed

2 to 4 cloves garlic, pressed or
   minced

1 tablespoon fresh ginger, finely
   minced

1 large red bell pepper, diced

2 tomatoes, diced

1/4 cup extra-virgin olive oil

3/4 teaspoon turmeric

Cayenne

5 slices of shepherd's French
   bread (or 1 baguette)

It's only appropriate that this eggplant dish is Indian, since India is where eggplant originated. From there it was domesticated in China, then taken to Africa, and later to Italy.

The beauty of eggplant is that it is filling but not fattening. Like other bland foods, it works well with any flavors you match it with, such as the exotic Asian spices used here.

1 sprinkle salt on eggplant cubes and toss. Let stand while the rest of the preparations take place.

2 sauté garlic and ginger in a little water for a couple of minutes over medium heat. Add red bell pepper and sauté until the pepper begins to soften.

3 add tomatoes and oil and continue to cook for another 5 to 10 minutes. Add spices and stir, going lightly on salt and cayenne until the end.

4 rinse salt off eggplant and add eggplant cubes to the rest of the mixture. Continue to cook until eggplant has softened to desired texture. Add water along the way to keep mixture from becoming too dry. Serve hot over grilled or broiled French bread or baguette cut lengthwise.

NOTE • the eggplant mixture also stands well alone as a side dish to curried rice, bean, or vegetable dishes.

- -

EYE-PLEASING SERVING SUGGESTIONS •

The primary rule of thumb in presenting an attractive meal is to add color. It's amazing how far a few slices of red tomatoes with a couple sprigs of herbs on the side of a dish can go in eye appeal. Here are some other simple ways to create attractive looking plates:

- *Place chopped, fresh herbs on top of bland looking soups.*
- *Place citrus wedges on the side of an entrée or side dish.*
- *Put composed or other non-green salads on a bed of crisp romaine or green leaf lettuce leaves.*
- *Use edible flowers on the plate or serving platter.*
- *Create bundles of julienned vegetables by tying them together with chives or green onions (this is especially beautiful with carrots).*
- *Use a single leaf of red chard, with part of the stem intact, as a beautiful background for salads, side dishes and entrees.*

- -

grilled garden sandwich

Serves 1

1/2 teaspoon butter (or vegetable
   oil cooking spray)

1 to 1 1/2 ounces sharp Cheddar
   cheese, sliced

2 slices sourdough bread (or your
   favorite bread)

6 to 8 slices cucumber

2 to 3 thin slices onion

2 to 3 slices tomato

2 tablespoons grated carrots

Lettuce leaf

Alfalfa sprouts

2 to 3 teaspoons dressing (equal
   parts mayonnaise and ketchup)

Thousand Island–type dressing gives this "salad on sourdough" sandwich an interesting twist.

1 heat skillet over medium heat. Add butter and brush over bottom of skillet when melted. Place cheese on top of 1 slice of bread. Grill both pieces of bread in skillet until cheese begins to melt.

2 begin layering vegetables on cheese. Spread dressing on other piece of bread and place on top of vegetables.

vegetarian reuben sandwich

Serves 1

3 tablespoons Bavarian Sauerkraut
  (page 199)

1/2 teaspoon butter (or vegetable
  oil spray)

1 teaspoon spicy mustard

1 slice of rye bread

1 ounce sliced Jarlsberg Swiss
  (or Swiss Alpine Lace cheese
  for a lowfat version)

1/4 avocado, sliced (or tomato
  slices for lowfat version)

Avocado takes the place of pastrami in this tasty, lighter version of the classic Reuben sandwich.

1 heat sauerkraut in a saucepan over medium heat.

2 heat skillet over medium heat and brush with butter. Spread mustard on bread. Place cheese on bread. Grill bread, covering skillet, until bread is golden on backside and cheese is melted on top. Remove from skillet.

3 layer avocado, then sauerkraut, on top and serve open-faced.

desserts

wine-poached pears with spiced ricotta

brandy-baked apples with custard sauce

fig bars

lemony scones

mocha ice milk

meyer lemon sorbet

"pumpkin pie" soup

old-world fruit crisp

strawberries with maple devonshire cream

strawberry sherbet with grand marnier

smoky ginger cookies

honey pound cake

plantation cookies

marty's banana bread

pineapple–coconut upside-down cake

fresh peach cobbler

wine-poached pears
with spiced ricotta

Serves 4

1 1/2 cups red wine

1/4 cup plus 2 tablespoons honey

2 tablespoons freshly squeezed
   lemon juice

4 small pears (any firm variety)

1/2 cup ricotta cheese

Cinnamon

Ideally you should find a firm variety of pear for poaching. Bosc pears, while appearing to be dry and hard, are actually quite juicy and aromatic after a couple of days on the shelf, and they poach nicely. In addition, they have a slender and elegant shape for presenting as a dessert.

Poached pears make a light and healthy finish to a meal and deliver a lot of flavor with virtually none of the sin.

1 heat wine in a small saucepan over medium heat. Add 2 tablespoons honey and 1 1/2 tablespoons lemon juice. Bring to a boil.

2 add peeled, cored, and halved pears to the wine, making sure all of the pear halves are covered in the wine mixture. Cover and simmer for 10 to 15 minutes, testing texture with a fork after 10 minutes. Do not allow pears to become mushy. Remove from wine when they've reached the desired texture.

3 bring wine back to a boil and add another 2 tablespoons honey. Continue to boil for 3 to 5 minutes, until the sauce thickens.

4 add 1/2 tablespoon lemon juice to ricotta along with 2 tablespoons honey and a generous pinch of cinnamon. Mix well.

5 place 2 pear halves in each dessert bowl with a dollop of ricotta in each half. Spoon wine sauce over the top. Serve warm.

VARIATION • *vanilla ice cream can be used in place of ricotta for a slightly more decadent dessert.*

brandy-baked apples
with custard sauce

Serves 4

BAKED APPLES

3 apples (a firm and tart variety)

1/4 cup brown sugar

Sprinkling salt

2 tablespoons freshly squeezed
lemon juice

1/3 cup brandy

CUSTARD SAUCE

1 egg, slightly beaten

1 1/2 cups whole milk

1/4 cup sugar

1 tablespoon cornstarch

1/8 teaspoon salt

1/2 teaspoon vanilla extract
(or 1 1/2 tablespoons brandy
or bourbon)

Fresh mint sprig or strawberry
(optional for garnish)

Custard was always a favorite of ours growing up, but with the mixed reviews eggs have received in recent years, custard has become a risky endeavor. Do not despair: This recipe uses whole milk in the place of a heavier cream and calls for only one egg. Divide that by four servings and you're home free.

1 slice and core apples and arrange in a 9-inch square glass baking dish.

2 sprinkle brown sugar, salt, lemon juice, and brandy evenly over apples.

3 microwave on high for 5 to 6 minutes, until apples are tender but not mushy.

4 to make custard sauce, mix egg and milk together.

5 put sugar, cornstarch, and 1/8 teaspoon salt in a saucepan over medium-low heat. Immediately add milk and egg slowly, stirring constantly. Add vanilla. Stir with whisk over medium-low heat until mixture thickens.

6 spoon 1/4 cup custard onto each of 4 dessert plates. Arrange baked apple slices on top of custard in a pinwheel pattern. Garnish with fresh mint sprig or strawberry in center.

fig bars

Makes 9 bars

FILLING

1 pound dried white figs, cut up

3/4 cup apple juice (preferably
   unsweetened and unfiltered)

1 tablespoon orange zest

CRUST

1/2 cup butter, softened

1/4 cup brown sugar

1/4 cup sugar

3/4 cup flour

1 cup ground walnuts

1/2 teaspoon ground cinnamon

1/4 teaspoon ground nutmeg

1 egg yolk, lightly beaten

TOPPING

3 tablespoons sugar

1/2 cup rolled oats

There was a time when fig Newtons were at the top of the list in my book. You'd scrape the coating off one side, then the other, leaving the wonderful chewy center—the reverse Oreo process.

The following recipe is a grown-up answer to those packaged childhood delights.

1 simmer figs in apple juice with orange zest until plump and moisture is absorbed. It only takes a few minutes.

2 while figs are simmering, mix all crust ingredients except egg yolk until mixture reaches an even granular texture. Divide mixture in half. Add egg yolk to half of mixture. Pat this mixture into bottom of 8 x 8-inch baking dish. Bake at 350 degrees F for 20 minutes. Remove from oven and spread cooked figs over crust.

3 add sugar and oats to other half of crust mixture. Sprinkle over figs and bake for another 20 minutes.

VARIATION • *the filling can be replaced with dates or another softened dried fruit such as apricots.*

lemony scones

Makes 8 scones

2 tablespoons butter

1/4 cup sugar

1 1/2 cups flour

1 tablespoon baking powder

1 tablespoon lemon zest

Dash of salt

1/2 cup plus 1 tablespoon whole
   milk

1/2 beaten egg

I first became a fan of scones while traveling in England. But as often happens, American chefs get their hands on classic dishes and begin improvising, giving an old favorite new meaning.

Pastry shops across the nation now offer an astounding variety of wonderful scones, but sometimes the simplest are the best. Paired with a little Devonshire cream (a mixture of whipped cream and sour cream) and jam or marmalade, these lemon-scented scones offer a classic afternoon tea experience.

1 cream together butter and sugar.

2 add flour and baking powder with a fork. Blend until mixture reaches a fine granulated texture with no noticeable lumps. Add lemon zest and salt.

3 add milk and egg and mix only until all dry ingredients are moistened, making sure not to overhandle dough.

4 with fingers, scoop 8 pieces of dough about the size of a lime onto a lightly oiled cookie sheet. Bake at 400 degrees F for 10 to 12 minutes until scones are firm and beginning to turn golden on the edges and top. Serve hot.

VARIATION • *omit lemon zest and use as the biscuit for fruit shortcakes. Split in the middle and scoop fruit onto bottom half, cover with other half, and top with more fruit. Top shortcake with whipped cream or ice cream if desired.*

mocha ice milk

Serves 4

2 1/2 cups whole milk

2/3 cup evaporated nonfat milk

1/2 cup sugar

1 tablespoon instant coffee

1 tablespoon unsweetened cocoa
  powder

2 tablespoons very hot water

Chocolate-covered espresso beans
  (optional)

The first time I made this lowfat ice cream recipe, the concoction never made it out of the ice cream maker. A tangle of sticky spoons and hands finished it off in minutes. The gang liked its rich flavor and refreshingly light texture.

1 combine milk, evaporated milk, and sugar until sugar dissolves.

2 dissolve coffee and cocoa powder in hot water, stirring until no lumps are present. Add to milk mixture. Put into an ice cream maker.

3 freeze using your favorite method of ice cream making. When frozen, remove from ice cream maker and put ice cream into a freezer-safe container. Freeze for 2 hours.

4 garnish with chocolate-covered espresso beans and serve.

meyer lemon sorbet

Serves 6

3/4 cup freshly squeezed Meyer
    lemon juice (less if using more
    bitter variety)

2 cups water

2/3 cup sugar

1/4 cup Triple Sec (optional)

Meyer lemons are known for their bright orangish-yellow flesh and full, somewhat sweet flavor. Try another backyard variety if possible, or reduce the amount of lemon juice if only very tart varieties can be found. If you like the tartness, you can also add a little more sugar.

1 mix all ingredients and pour into ice cream maker.

2 use your favorite ice cream making method to freeze sorbet. Serve immediately or freeze.

EDIBLE FLOWERS • *Create a wonderful food presentation using edible flowers. Beautiful blossoms can be found in the garden or packaged in gourmet shops—for a price. They add magnificent beauty and color to even the blandest looking dish, as well as some complex and interesting flavors. One easy way to experiment with edible flowers is in salads. Here are some of the more common edible flowers: calendula, lavender, borage, scented geranium, roses, pansies, violets, impatiens, mint flowers, and squash blossoms.*

"pumpkin pie" soup

Serves 4 to 6

1 can (16 ounces) pumpkin

1 1/2 cups evaporated milk

1 1/2 cups lowfat cow's milk
  (or soy milk)

1/4 cup freshly squeezed tangerine
  juice (or orange juice)

2 tablespoons bourbon (or brandy)

1/4 teaspoon cloves

1/4 teaspoon ginger

1/2 teaspoon cinnamon

3/4 teaspoon coriander

2 tablespoons sugar

Salt

If you've ever made a pumpkin pie, you may have found yourself sampling the soupy mixture along the way, maybe even licking the bowl clean. Like cookie dough, pumpkin pie batter tastes better to some of us than the finished product. Because this mixture is much too wonderful to limit to one or two pies a year, I decided to turn it into a soup that could be eaten throughout the winter. This soup would be perfect served in small portions and paired with a Sunday brunch on a cold day.

1 put pumpkin in saucepan over medium-low heat. Add milks (you may need to add more than the recipe calls for to reach desired consistency). Add tangerine juice and bourbon. Add spices.

2 add sugar, tasting as you go until you reach the desired level of sweetness. Add salt to taste. Serve hot.

SERVING SUGGESTION • *serve in small portions with a dollop of whipped cream if desired.*

old-world fruit crisp

Serves 6

4 cups sliced fruit (apples, peaches,
    pears, or berries)
1 1/2 tablespoons fresh lemon juice
Salt
1/2 cup firmly packed brown sugar
1/2 cup flour
1/4 cup softened butter (add salt if
    unsalted butter is used)
1/2 cup rolled oats
1/2 teaspoon cinnamon
Zest of 1 lemon
1/4 cup finely chopped walnuts
    (optional)

Is there any dish more representative of hearth and home than a fruit crisp? Always a favorite, use your favorite fruit to create your own version of this classic American dessert. Be careful to take the texture of the fruit into account while baking, making sure not to overcook the fruit.

1 place fruit in bottom of an 8-inch square baking pan or 8-inch pie tin. Sprinkle with lemon juice and a little salt, tossing for an even coating.

2 mix sugar and flour together. Add butter and mix until crumbly. Add oats, cinnamon, lemon zest, and walnuts (if using) and work until well mixed and crumbly.

3 sprinkle topping over fruit and bake at 350 degrees F for 20 to 30 minutes, depending on the firmness of the fruit. Serve hot or at room temperature.

strawberries with maple devonshire cream

1 quart fresh strawberries
(2 baskets)

1 1/2 cups whipped cream
(preferably homemade)

1/3 cup sour cream

1/4 teaspoon plus a few drops
maple flavoring

1 1/2 tablespoons packed brown
sugar

There is something wonderfully decadent about dipping desserts. Here, strawberries are paired with a maple-scented cream for a simple yet elegant dessert perfect for parties and romantic get-togethers.

1 wash strawberries and allow them to dry in a colander or strainer.

2 mix whipped cream and sour cream until smooth. Add maple flavoring and brown sugar, making sure to crumble any lumps in the sugar before adding it to the cream.

3 serve cream in one bowl and strawberries in another, family style, with a separate bowl on the table for the discarded strawberry caps.

strawberry sherbet
with grand marnier

Serves 4

1 egg white

3 cups strawberries, washed and
   hulled

1/3 cup sugar

2 tablespoons Grand Marnier

1/3 cup half-and-half

2 cantaloupes (if in season)

Grand Marnier gives this strawberry sherbet an elegant twist, but is not essential if you are serving to minors or those who do not partake. To put the full flavor of summer into this refreshing treat, be sure to use sun-ripened local berries. Serve with biscotti or butter cookies.

1 beat egg white until soft peaks form.

2 purée strawberries in a food processor until mostly smooth but with a little texture left.

3 fold strawberries into egg whites. Fold in sugar and Grand Marnier. Fold in half-and-half.

4 freeze in your ice cream maker using your favorite freezing method. Transfer to freezer-safe container and freeze for 1 to 2 hours to allow sherbet to set up.

5 cut cantaloupes in half and scoop out pulp and seeds. Scoop sherbet into center and serve.

smoky ginger cookies

Makes 3 dozen cookies

3/4 cup butter, softened

1 cup sugar

1/4 cup dark molasses

1 large egg

2 cups unbleached white flour

1/4 teaspoon salt

1/4 teaspoon hickory salt

2 teaspoons baking soda

1 teaspoon ground ginger

3/4 teaspoon ground cloves

1 teaspoon cinnamon

Extra sugar for rolling

On a snowy night in Lake Tahoe during the holiday season, I made these smoky, spicy cookies for four adults. By the end of the evening we had eaten the entire batch—that's how addictive these cookies are.

1 heat oven to 350 degrees F. Cream butter and sugar together until smooth. Add molasses and continue to stir until smooth. Add remaining ingredients, except extra sugar.

2 pinch off walnut-size pieces of dough and roll in hands. Roll in sugar until lightly coated. Place on greased baking sheet and press flat with fingers.

3 bake for 10 to 12 minutes.

honey pound cake

Makes 1 loaf

2 cups unbleached white flour

1/2 teaspoon salt

2 teaspoons baking powder

3/4 cup softened butter

3/4 cup sugar

3/4 cup honey

4 eggs

1/3 cup milk

2 teaspoons vanilla

Zest of 2 lemons

Confectioners' sugar

This traditional dense and moist cake uses honey and lemon zest to augment the otherwise subtle flavor. As one of the most versatile desserts, pound cake can be served with fruit, sorbet, or ice cream and drizzled with chocolate or fruit purée or even served by itself.

1 sift together flour, salt, and baking powder.

2 cream together butter and sugar until smooth. Add honey and continue to blend.

3 add eggs, one at a time.

4 add milk alternately with dry ingredients and mix until smooth.

5 add vanilla and lemon zest.

6 bake in loaf pan at 325 degrees F for 1 hour and 10 minutes, until toothpick inserted in center comes out clean.

7 sprinkle with confectioners' sugar. Cool, turn out of baking dish, slice, and serve with your favorite topping or alone.

plantation cookies

Makes about 30 cookies

1/2 cup butter

2/3 cup brown sugar

1/3 cup sugar

1 egg

2 tablespoons water

1/2 teaspoon vanilla extract

1 cup unbleached white flour

1/2 teaspoon baking soda

1/4 teaspoon salt

1 teaspoon allspice

1/2 teaspoon cinnamon

1 cup oats

1 cup firmly packed shredded
  coconut

2/3 cup golden raisins

2/3 cup halved macadamia nuts
  (or walnuts or pecans)

I ran across a Hawaiian version of Mrs. Field's cookies while on vacation in the islands. Macadamia nuts give these chewy delights a rich and crunchy texture, but can be replaced with walnuts or pecans.

1 cream together butter and sugars. Add egg, beating until smooth. Add water and vanilla extract and continue to beat until smooth.

2 add flour, baking soda, salt, allspice, and cinnamon and stir until all flour is absorbed and a soft dough is formed. Add oats, coconut, raisins, and nuts and stir until evenly distributed.

3 bake on greased baking sheet at 350 degrees F for 12 to 14 minutes.

marty's banana bread

Makes 1 loaf

3 ripe bananas

1/2 cup butter

1 cup sugar

2 eggs

1 cup unbleached white flour

1 cup whole wheat flour

1 teaspoon baking soda

1/2 teaspoon salt

1/3 cup hot water

1/2 cup walnuts

1/2 cup raisins

A friend of mine passed this recipe along to me 20 years ago, and while I never even learned Marty's last name, her banana bread recipe remains the best I've tasted to this day. Thanks, Marty, wherever you are.

1 mash bananas with a fork until mostly smooth but with some texture remaining.

2 melt butter in a medium saucepan over low heat. Remove from heat and add sugar, stirring until well blended. Add eggs and mix until smooth. Add bananas and mix well.

3 in another bowl, mix dry ingredients. Begin adding to banana mixture slowly, alternating with hot water. Stir until smooth. Add nuts and raisins.

4 bake in a buttered loaf pan at 325 degrees F for 1 hour to 1 hour and 15 minutes, depending on oven and loaf pan used. Bread is done when toothpick inserted in center comes out clean. Remove from oven and cool for a couple of hours before slicing and serving.

pineapple–coconut upside-down cake

Serves 12

TOPPING

1/4 cup cold butter, cut into small
　　pieces

1 cup moderately packed brown
　　sugar

1 cup shredded coconut

2 cups pineapple chunks, drained
　　and cut into smaller pieces

CAKE

1 2/3 cups unbleached white flour

1 cup sugar

1/2 teaspoon salt

2 teaspoons baking powder

1/2 cup butter, softened

2 eggs

1/2 cup buttermilk

1/3 cup milk

1 teaspoon almond extract (or
　　vanilla extract)

This upside-down cake can be made with any fruit you like, depending on what's in season. Try plums, peaches, or berries. Add a splash of liqueur if you like. All of these options complement this moist, almond-scented cake.

1 heat oven to 350 degrees F.

2 place pieces of butter evenly along bottom of 9 × 13-inch baking dish. Sprinkle brown sugar over butter. Sprinkle coconut over sugar. Place pineapple pieces evenly over sugar and butter.

3 to make cake, mix flour, sugar, salt, and baking powder. Add all other ingredients and mix with electric mixer on low for 30 seconds, then on high for another 1 minute 30 seconds.

4 gently pour batter over fruit and bake for 30 minutes. Cake is done when toothpick inserted in center comes out clean. Cool and serve.

fresh peach cobbler

Serves 6

5 peaches, skinned and thinly
sliced

1/4 cup sugar

Juice of 1/2 lemon

Salt

1 to 2 tablespoons cold butter, cut
into small pieces

Cinnamon (optional)

1/2 batch Lemony Scones, omit-
ting the lemon zest if desired
(page 274)

When you've overpicked or overbought those juicy, sweet globes of summer, make this cobbler before they soften and wither before your eyes.

1 heat oven to 400 degrees F.

2 place sliced peaches in a 9-inch square baking dish. Mix in sugar, lemon juice, and a sprinkling of salt. Place butter pieces evenly among the peaches. Sprinkle with cinnamon as desired.

3 divide scone batter into 4 parts and spoon on top of fruit, spreading out with fingers for better coverage.

4 bake for 25 minutes or until golden on top. Serve warm or at room temperature.

NOTE • don't allow cobbler to sit too long before serving as the top biscuit will become soft and doughy.

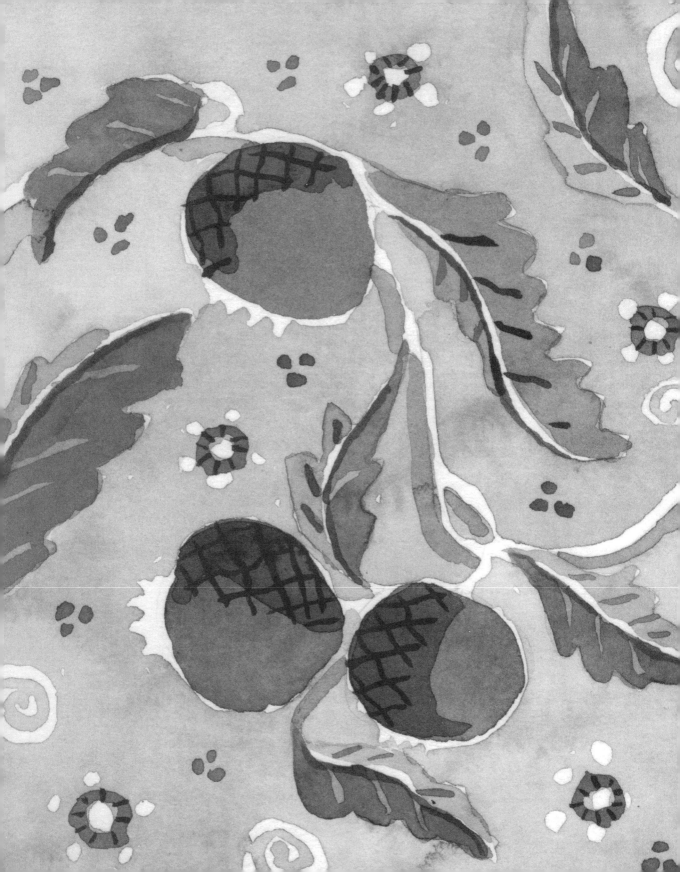

smoothies and beverages

fruit protein smoothie

orange dream

chocolate monkey

cherry almond delight

date–walnut smoothie

almond milk

fresh ginger lemonade

cow, goat, and soy milks

A milk comparison table is provided on page 291 to help you when evaluating your protein sources for morning drinks. If you are watching your cholesterol levels, for example, you may find soy milk a better alternative than cow's milk. Goat's milk is often more easily digestible for people with lactose intolerance. Cow's milk, meanwhile, provides a greater amount of protein than the other types.

You'll notice that most of these smoothies are milk based or protein fortified. This is because the intent of these morning smoothies is to give you a solid protein base to start the day. The result will be a more sustained energy level throughout the morning. You may even notice that the mid-morning slump disappears.

In the table on page 291, you will also notice an entry for lowfat cottage cheese. Cottage cheese is one of the best foods available to lacto-ovo vegetarians in terms of a calorie-and-fat to protein ratio. It's a mainstay for me when a steady energy level is needed, or for those watching their weight.

A COMPARISON OF MILKS

Type	Calories	Protein	Fat	Carbohydrates
Cow's (whole)	160	8 g	8 g	13 g
Cow's (1%)	120	10 g	2.5 g	16 g
Goat's (whole)	140	8 g	7 g	11 g
Goat's (1%)	90	7 g	2.5 g	9 g
Soy (whole)	160	9 g	7 g	14 g
Soy (1%)	80	4 g	2.5 g	15 g
Rice (1%)	120	2 g	1 g	25 g
Cottage Cheese (1/2 cup lowfat)	90	14 g	2 g	5 g

fruit protein smoothie

Serves 1

1/2 cup orange juice

1 (3-inch) length of banana

3 to 4 strawberries

1/3 cup yogurt

1 tablespoon protein powder
(optional)

1 to 2 teaspoons honey, or grade B
or C pure maple syrup

2 ice cubes

blend all ingredients until smooth.

----

*USING SMOOTHIES AS A DISGUISE FOR
HEALTHFUL INGREDIENTS* • *Even when my son passed the six
foot mark, I was up concocting his morning smoothies before school. This is an excellent
opportunity to slip healthful substances into their growing bodies without their knowledge.
In addition to the ingredients found in the smoothies, I'll often add other super-charged
ingredients such as powdered vitamin C during cold season, an omega-3 and omega-6 rich
oil blend, protein powder—whatever Dr. Mom thinks his body needs. That way when he
trades off all of the healthful foods in his lunch for Snickers bars, he'll still have something
to go on.*

----

orange dream

Serves 1

6 ounces orange juice

1 tablespoon protein powder (or
   2 tablespoons powdered milk)

1 to 2 teaspoons granulated fructose (or sugar)

1/2 teaspoon vanilla extract

3 ice cubes

2 tablespoons egg substitute
   (optional)

blend all ingredients until smooth.

chocolate monkey

Serves 1

6 ounces milk

1/2 banana

1 tablespoon protein powder (or
   2 tablespoons powdered milk)

2 tablespoons raw almonds (or
   walnut pieces)

1 teaspoon cocoa powder

2 teaspoons honey, granulated
   fructose, or grade B or C pure
   maple syrup

3 ice cubes

blend all ingredients until smooth.

cherry almond delight

Serves 1

1/4 cup yogurt

1/2 cup milk

1/4 cup pitted cherries (fresh or
　 frozen)

12 to 14 raw almonds

1/2 teaspoon vanilla extract

1 teaspoon granulated fructose,
　 honey, or grade B or C pure
　 maple syrup

3 ice cubes

blend all ingredients until smooth.

USING FROZEN AND CANNED PRODUCE •

There are times when it is appropriate to use frozen or canned produce rather than fresh. If you live in a region that has limited fresh produce in the winter or if you confine your meals to those varieties of produce grown seasonally in your region, then you may get better flavor from frozen or canned produce. Why? Produce is often shipped long distances and stored in distribution centers before it hits the produce aisle, which means it can be over-the-hill in freshness, or it may have been picked before it was ripe to survive the journey. This is where frozen or canned produce is better. Both have been processed quickly after harvest to preserve the peak of freshness and flavor. For example, I often suggest using canned tomatoes in place of fresh unless you have access to vine-ripened tomatoes. While vine-ripened tomatoes are now more accessible year-round due to hot house growers, they are on the expensive side.

---

date–walnut smoothie

Serves 1

6 ounces milk

1 tablespoon powdered milk

2 to 3 large dates (soft variety),
   pits removed

2 tablespoons walnut pieces

1/4 teaspoon vanilla extract

3 ice cubes

2 tablespoons egg substitute
   (optional)

blend all ingredients until smooth.

almond milk

Serves 1

6 ounces milk

12 to 14 raw almonds

1 to 2 teaspoons honey, or grade B
   or C pure maple syrup

Pinch of cinnamon

Pinch of nutmeg

Pinch of freshly ground black pepper

1 to 2 ice cubes (optional)

This recipe is based on an Ayurvedic recipe designed to sustain an even energy level for hours. Black pepper and nutmeg give this drink its unique flavor. Almonds are considered to be the perfect food for balanced saturated and unsaturated fats. This is a personal favorite of mine for both flavor and health benefits, especially if you're feeling stressed or scattered.

blend all ingredients until smooth. Add ice cube toward the end of blending, as it takes a little extra time for the almonds to grind.

fresh ginger lemonade

Serves 1

1 teaspoon pressed fresh ginger

Juice of 1 lemon

2 tablespoons grade B or C maple
    syrup (see note)

Dash of cayenne pepper

1/2 to 3/4 cup spring or filtered
    water (or sparkling mineral
    water)

When your body is feeling tired and polluted, reach for this drink instead of coffee and you will be doing yourself a big favor. It has all of the energy-lifting effects without the crash and health-robbing effects of caffeine. It also tastes great!

1 cut the ginger into small pieces and press in a garlic press, allowing the juice to fall into a glass. You may have to do this a couple of times depending on how dry or moist the ginger is. Try to use the freshest ginger with a smooth, thin skin.

2 blend all remaining ingredients with the ginger juice. A sante!

NOTE • grade B maple syrup is less processed and has all of the full flavor and most of the nutrients of raw syrup. Use it as you would any other maple syrup.

index

d

e

International Conversion Chart

These are not exact equivalents: they have been slightly rounded to make measuring easier.

LIQUID MEASUREMENTS

American	Imperial	Metric	Australian
2 tablespoons (1 oz.)	1 fl. oz.	30 ml	1 tablespoon
1/4 cup (2 oz.)	2 fl. oz.	60 ml	2 tablespoons
1/3 cup (3 oz.)	3 fl. oz.	80 ml	1/4 cup
1/2 cup (4 oz.)	4 fl. oz.	125 ml	1/3 cup
2/3 cup (5 oz.)	5 fl. oz.	165 ml	1/2 cup
3/4 cup (6 oz.)	6 fl. oz.	185 ml	2/3 cup
1 cup (8 oz.)	8 fl. oz.	250 ml	3/4 cup

SPOON MEASUREMENTS

American	Metric
1/4 teaspoon	1 ml
1/2 teaspoon	2 ml
1 teaspoon	5 ml
1 tablespoon	15 ml

WEIGHTS

US/UK	Metric
1 oz.	30 grams (g)
2 oz.	60 g
4 oz. (1/4 lb)	125 g
5 oz. (1/3 lb)	155 g
6 oz.	185 g
7 oz.	220 g
8 oz. (1/2 lb)	250 g
10 oz.	315 g
12 oz. (3/4 lb)	375 g
14 oz.	440 g
16 oz. (1 lb)	500 g
2 lbs	1 kg

OVEN TEMPERATURES

Farenheit	Centigrade	Gas
250	120	1/2
300	150	2
325	160	3
350	180	4
375	190	5
400	200	6
450	230	8